THE
GOSPEL
FOR LIFE
SERIES

THE GOSPEL &

Abortion

Also in the *Gospel for Life* series

THE
GOSPEL
FOR LIFE

—— SERIES ——

THE GOSPEL &

Abortion

SERIES EDITORS

RUSSELL MOORE *and*
ANDREW T. WALKER

PUBLISHING GROUP

NASHVILLE, TENNESSEE

Published by B&H Publishing Group
Nashville, Tennessee

Dewey Decimal Classification: 241.69
Subject Heading: BIBLE. N.T. GOSPELS \
ABORTION \ LIFE

1 2 3 4 5 6 7 8 • 21 20 19 18 17

CONTENTS

Series Preface

Russell Moore

Why Should the *Gospel for Life* Series Matter to Churches?

IN ACTS CHAPTER 2, WE READ ABOUT THE DAY OF PENTECOST, the day when the resurrected Lord Jesus Christ sent the Holy Spirit from heaven onto His church. The Day of Pentecost was a spectacular day—there were manifestations of fire, languages being spoken by people who didn't know them, and thousands of unbelievers coming to faith in this recently resurrected Messiah. Reading this passage, we go from account to account of heavenly shock and awe, and yet the passage ends in an unexpectedly simple way: "And they devoted themselves to the apostles' teaching and the fellowship, to the breaking of bread and the prayers" (Acts 2:42 ESV).

I believe one thing the Holy Spirit wants us to understand from this is that these "ordinary" things are not less spectacular than what preceded them—in fact, they may be more so. The disciplines of discipleship, fellowship, community, and prayer are the signs that tell us the kingdom of Christ is here. That means that for Christians, the most crucial moments in our walk with Jesus Christ don't happen in the thrill of "spiritual highs." They happen in the common hum of everyday life in quiet, faithful obedience to Christ.

That's what the *Gospel for Life* series is about: taking the truths of Scripture—the story of our redemption and adoption by a risen Lord Jesus—and applying them to the questions and situations that we all face in the ordinary course of life.

Our hope is that churches will not merely find these books interesting, but also helpful. The *Gospel for Life* series is meant to assist pastors and church leaders to answer urgent questions that people are asking, questions that the church isn't always immediately ready to answer. Whether in a counseling session or alongside a sermon series, these books are intended to come alongside church leaders in discipling members to see their lives with a Kingdom mentality.

Believers don't live the Christian life in isolation but rather as part of a gospel community, the church. That's why we have structured the *Gospel for Life* series to be easily utilized in anything from a small group study context to a new member or new believer class. None of us can live worthy of the gospel by ourselves and, thankfully, none have to.

Why are we so preoccupied with the idea of living life by and through the gospel? The answer is actually quite simple: because the gospel changes everything. The gospel isn't a mere theological inquiry or a political idea, though it shapes both our theology and our politics. The gospel is the Good News that there is a Kingdom far above and beyond the borders of this world, where death is dead and sin and sorrow cease. The gospel is about how God brings this Kingdom to us by reconciling us to Himself through Christ.

That means two things. First, it means the gospel fulfills the hopes that our idols have promised and betrayed. The Scripture says that all God's promises are yes in Jesus (2 Cor. 1:20). As sinful human beings, we all tend to think what we really want is freedom from authority, inheritance without obedience like the prodigal son. But what Jesus offers is the authority we were designed to live under, an inheritance we by no means deserve to share, and the freedom that truly satisfies our souls.

Second, this means that the gospel isn't just the start of the Christian life but rather the vehicle that carries it along. The gospel is about the daily reality of living as an adopted child of a resurrected Father-King, whose Kingdom is here and is still coming. By looking at our jobs, our marriages, our families, our government, and the entire universe through a gospel lens, we live differently. We will work and marry and vote with a Kingdom mind-set, one that prioritizes the permanent things of

Christ above the fleeting pleasures of sin and the vaporous things of this world.

The *Gospel for Life* series is about helping Christians and churches navigate life in the Kingdom while we wait for the return of its king and its ultimate consummation. The stakes are high. To get the gospel wrong when it comes to marriage can lead to a generation's worth of confusion about what marriage even is. To get the gospel wrong on adoption can leave millions of "unwanted" children at the mercy of ruthless sex traffickers and callous abusers. There's no safe space in the universe where getting the gospel wrong will be merely an academic blunder. That's why these books exist—to help you and your church understand what the gospel is and what it means for life.

Theology doesn't just think; it walks, weeps, and bleeds. The *Gospel for Life* series is a resource intended to help Christians see their theology do just that. When you see all of life from the perspective of the Kingdom, everything changes. It's not just about miraculous moments or intense religious experiences. Our gospel is indeed miraculous, but as the disciples in Acts learned, it's also a gospel of the ordinary.

Introduction

Andrew T. Walker

AS MUCH AS ABORTION IS A HUMAN RIGHTS ISSUE, IT'S A GOSPEL issue.

As Christians, we aren't called to view every action or controversial issue only through the grid of culture or politics. Some issues—like abortion—transcend the political. In turn, we're called to see all of life underneath the lordship of Jesus Christ and His rightful authority over every human life.

It's a topic that touches every sphere of our existence. It affects the mother who has chosen to abort and can't shake the guilt and accusation that inflicts her conscience. It affects the father who will never know his child. It affects local churches as they attempt to foster a culture of life in their communities. Abortion affects the political arena as pro-life citizens work to see our laws protect the most vulnerable.

As a human dignity issue, abortion is the preeminent human rights problem of our time. When taking scope of what the

United States Supreme Court did in its 1973 *Roe v. Wade* decision, the carnage of human life left in its aftermath is simply incalculable. A generation of Americans has been snuffed out of existence.

Every abortion robs God of His glory by putting man and government in place of God, determining life and death. As Russell Moore often writes, "There is no one more pro-choice than Satan when a woman walks into an abortion clinic; and there is no one more pro-life than Satan after a woman walks out of an abortion clinic." Deceit and accusation are the most powerful tools in his arsenal against us. But those in Christ have something more: we have forgiveness, redemption, and the promise of Christ's perfect righteousness. When Christians face abortion, just like they face any other issue, they face it with one truth: the gospel of Jesus Christ.

We're pleased to present you with *The Gospel and Abortion*. This book is intended to be an introductory look at how Christians should engage this controversial topic from every angle of the Christian life—their place in culture, their engagement as everyday Christians, and their role in the body of Christ—the church. We want no stone left unturned when talking about how the gospel of Jesus Christ shapes us as a people on mission for God in every sphere of our life—not least of which is the protection of unborn life, the one institution in which most people will find themselves for forty to even sixty years.

Each book in the *Gospel for Life* series is structured the same: What are we for? What does the gospel say? How should the Christian live? How should the church engage? What does the culture say?

It's our prayer that as you read this book, the Spirit of Christ will open your hearts to how the gospel informs the abortion debate in America, and why, as Christians have testified from their earliest beginnings, abortion isn't just an "issue" for Christians. Abortion speaks to the very core of our belief—that God is the Creator, and that every life—born and unborn—has intrinsic dignity because of God's imprint of His image upon them.

Are You Considering an Abortion?

Dear Friend,

I am writing to you as someone who has been where you are: deciding whether to abort or carry your baby. At the tender age of eighteen, I made a decision that would dramatically alter the rest of my life: I had an abortion. I would like to share with you all the things I wish I had known before I made that tragic decision.

I wish I had the wisdom to carefully examine the decision to abort and what it would not only cost me, but also cost the baby I was carrying. I made a decision out of fear: fear of rejection, fear of condemnation, fear of pregnancy, and fear of being alone. When we make a decision out of fear, we are completely self-focused. But this decision was not just about my life, but the life of my first child. I later realized that it was a decision that also affected the father of that baby as well as the baby's future siblings. One life touches so many.

I wish I would have known how much I already loved my baby. I was intimately connected to him and didn't fully realize it until the moment he was gone. You see, God has designed every woman to nurture and protect her children, not to kill them.

My suffering for the loss of that baby began immediately following the abortion. I allowed myself to believe a lie, that I was making a decision about a "pregnancy," not whether or not my child would live or die. I further allowed myself to believe that my baby wasn't really a baby yet. I had my abortion when I was just 6 weeks along, but I did not know that my baby's heart was beating at between 100 and 160 beats per minute, and that his own blood was already coursing through his own body as all of his organs were forming. I allowed myself to believe the lie that my baby was only a clump of tissue because believing the truth would be unthinkable.

Having an abortion almost destroyed my life. The loneliness I felt when my baby was gone was almost unbearable. I cried every day . . . for years. I became depressed and started experiencing headaches due to the tremendous guilt and anguish I experienced over what I had done. God did step in and heal me emotionally, physically, and spiritually when I repented and turned to Him for forgiveness. However, thirty-three years later, having raised four beautiful children that God so mercifully blessed me with, I can tell you that not a day goes by that I don't think of my first child that I aborted. Every year I remember the day and month he was aborted and on his would-have-been birth month, I imagine how old he would be.

I can never undo taking his life through abortion, but I can use his short life here on Earth in my womb as a testimony that his life mattered. My hope is that through our story, you will see how much your baby's life matters to you and to all the lives he will have the opportunity to touch if you allow him to live.

A Fellow Mother

CHAPTER

1

What Are We For?

Jim Hamilton

IF YOUR EXAMINATION OF THE BIBLE IS ONLY SURFACE LEVEL, when you come to a question like the one addressed in this chapter, you might conclude that the Bible says nothing about abortion. You could come to this conclusion from looking at the concordance in the back of a Bible and seeing no entry for the word *abortion*. You might even press a little further by going to a website such as BibleGateway.com and search the NIV for the word *abortion*, get no hits, and have your unfortunate conclusion reinforced.

Such a conclusion, arrived at in such a way, is as tragic as it is shallow. This method of determining what the Bible teaches would also lead one to think that the Bible says nothing about the Trinity or the two natures of Christ, that it says nothing about original sin, and that it pronounces no prohibition on pornography or mind-altering drugs, all because those specific words are not used. The Bible has clear teaching on all these issues, and the Bible's teaching can be applied to every possible ethical question people face.

The truth is that the Bible isn't silent on the issue of abortion. We know this because the Bible is not silent about the value of human life. At its deepest levels the Bible celebrates the birth of children. Scripture teaches that every person is created in the image of God and that every life is precious and miraculous. The celebration of new life lies at the heart of the biblical message heralding the triumph of life over death. So it is misguided to say the Bible doesn't speak to the abortion issue. It does, and its message is clear.

The thesis of this chapter is very simple: God is a God of life, and according to the Bible's inner logic, every human life is sacred and abortion is evil—in the same way that murder is evil. And we can go one step further and say this: in the Bible, were there no childbirth, there would be no salvation.

To justify these assertions, we have to set forth the Bible's inner logic. To do that, we need to look at specific statements and how they fit in the Bible's wider narrative. Prior to that, however, there are certain emotional realities to which we should allow the Bible to speak. The emotional realities I have in mind are the sorts of appeals that advocates of abortion use to deploy compassion—a biblical virtue—as a weapon in the war to justify something the Bible condemns: abortion.

Let me make one other, perhaps more personal, comment about emotions and abortion. Perhaps you yourself have had an abortion, or maybe you supported someone dear to you through an abortion. I understand the apprehension you may feel about reading further. Any consideration of this issue will be painful. There is hope for you, though, because pain often leads to healing.

Healing from spiritual and emotional pain can only happen by God's grace as a result of repentance. If you are going to get better, you are going to have to look this full in the face and see there all the ugliness of the evil you have done.

Proverbs 28:13 states, "The one who conceals his sins will not prosper, but whoever confesses and renounces them will find mercy."

There is no sin that the blood of Jesus cannot cover. He died on the cross to pay the penalty for sin. The only way for you to make progress on this issue will be for you to repent of all your sin, including abortion, and trust in Christ. In Christ, you will find forgiveness, mercy, and grace. In Christ, you will find peace and hope. And in Christ, you will find freedom from the weight and burden of all your sin. Everything that follows in this essay is designed to help you do that.

The Bible Is for Neighbor, God's Image, Dignity, and Least of These

Before making the case for the Bible's view of human dignity, I must respond to several common questions about abortion. In this section, I will address the topic of abortion from a biblical perspective, and some of these arguments will be further developed later in the chapter.

According to the Bible, God made the world and its rules, and those rules forbid abortion. God's rules are not unnecessary restrictions that keep good things from people. Rather, God's rules are the kind of loving boundaries parents put up around their little children to protect them from ways they could get hurt. God's laws forbid things that are bad for people. God's commandments, instructions, prohibitions, and teachings promote what is best for us: love for God and neighbor.

We are called to love our neighbors. The Bible's perspective on love for neighbor can be boiled down to the golden rule: do unto others as you would have them do unto you (Matt. 7:12). Who would want to be slain before they ever left the womb of their mother? There is no golden rule way to defend abortion. Abortion necessarily prevents us from showing love to others.

Furthermore, Christians also oppose abortion because we affirm that the following: the Bible teaches that humans are made in God's image and are thereby endowed with sacred dignity (Gen. 1:26–28); that human life begins at conception (see the discussion of Jer. 1:5 and Ps. 139 below); and that a death warrant cannot be put out on a person because of their size, level of development, environment, or degree of dependency.

Sometimes people defend their support for abortion by asking these kinds of questions:

1. Should a child, a daughter, for instance, be punished for a mistake?
2. What about the health of the mother?
3. What about cases of rape or incest?
4. What about the back-alley abortions that will happen anyway?

We will consider these one by one.

1. Should a child, a daughter, for instance, be punished for a mistake?

The problem with the reasoning reflected here is simply that it does not take into consideration all the children involved. In this scenario, the would-be grandfather/grandmother inexplicably considers his/her child, but not the grandchild. Christians recognize that both lives—the mother and child—are precious in God's sight and worthy of protection.

What kind of grandfather, for example, would have his grandchild killed rather than cause difficulty for his child? A pregnant child will face difficulties, but that does not warrant the execution of the child in the womb.

While we understand the impulse to protect one's child, this approach to parenting is clearly sinful: instead of a father leading his daughter to take responsibility for her actions, he seeks to get her off the hook by sanctioning the death of her child. Of course fathers should teach their children to save sexual intimacy for the marriage bed, but fathers should also teach their children that the conception of a child is a miraculous gift to be celebrated. Circumstances do not determine the value of a human life or the wonder of its existence.

2. What about the health of the mother?

Life-threatening cases are tragic and sometimes come with very difficult choices. But in these cases, we should promote medicine aimed to preserve life. We must not default to a position of ending one life to promote the other. Instead, we encourage physicians to make every attempt to save all lives involved.

3. What about cases of rape or incest?

Again, in these cases pregnancies sometimes arise from tragic circumstances. And victims of rape or incest certainly deserve our compassion. But to answer this question, we must ask another question: is it permissible to punish a child for a sin they did not commit? In no other instance would we give a death sentence to a child, especially not one that bears no moral culpability. No, we would insist that even in these instances, the life of the unborn child is valuable and fully deserving of protection.

4. What about the back-alley abortions that will happen anyway?

This line of reasoning will not stand up to scrutiny. If we recognize that the unborn life is a human being, there is no reason to deny him or her full legal protection. It is certainly regrettable that an unplanned pregnancy might cause such distress in certain cases, but this too is insufficient grounds to sanction the deaths of millions of children.

Though these appeals to emotion weigh heavy on our hearts and minds, they can never justify giving the death penalty to an innocent child in the womb of his or her mother. Unfortunately, these arguments often distract people from the real issue, namely that abortion is nothing less than ending an innocent human life. These questions may appeal to human kindness and decency, but they contradict themselves and distort reality. If we truly desire to live in service to our fellow man, we must recognize that abortion is an obstacle to this task. We deem others worthy of our kindness and respect because of our common humanity, yet we undermine this very truth by denying the personhood of the unborn. In our day, truly being people of kindness and decency is directly related to our affirmation of the dignity of every human life.

The Bible's Inner Logic: God Is for His Creation

Psalm 24:1 says, "The earth and everything in it, the world and its inhabitants, belong to the LORD." The assertion that all territory and all life—all life, even the unborn—belong to the God of the Bible stands on the psalm's next statement. Psalm 24:1–2 celebrates God as the Creator of the world and everything in it. Psalm 24:1 says God owns all, because we are told in Psalm 24:2 that God created all. The Bible's logic is simple: since God made the world, everything belongs to Him; and the fact that He made and owns everything further grants Him the right to make the rules. God is King, Lawgiver, Judge, and Savior (Isa. 33:22).

Under these premises, as the only giver of life, God is the only one with the right either to take life or to authorize its taking by others. God was so serious about life that at first He only authorized people and animals to eat plants (Gen. 1:30). After the flood, however, he authorized men to eat the meat of animals (9:3), though not meat containing the blood of life (9:4). And there is nothing more precious in all of God's good creation than human life. This is why, after the flood, God also authorized humans to put murderers to death: "Whoever sheds man's blood, his blood will be shed by man, for God made man in His image"

(9:6). Human beings bear and reflect the image of God. Humans are valuable because God is valuable. And protecting the image is paramount. For this reason the apostle Paul, writing in a new covenant context, endorses the right of human governments to visit capital punishment upon those who would eliminate or defile an image bearer in Romans 13:4.

Christians affirm the dignity of every person and uphold the value of every life precisely because of our belief that humans are made in the image of God. We also believe that murder is wrong because it demonstrates flagrant disregard for human life. For Christians, both justice and love of neighbor require us to stand firm in these beliefs.

Someone may object that all of this about life is well and good, but what about the question of when life begins? Is this unborn child merely a clump of cells? Are we dealing with a fetus or are we dealing with a human being made in the image of God? Does the Bible extend the human status of one made in the image of God to the unborn?

The answer to this question is yes, and that yes can be defended on a number of levels.

At a theological level, God says to Jeremiah, "Before I formed you in the womb I knew you, and before you were born I consecrated you" (Jer. 1:5 ESV). The first word of this statement, *Before,* shows that God knew Jeremiah prior to his conception, prior to the time Jeremiah spent in his mother's womb. This indicates that God knew Jeremiah before Jeremiah's father begot him. Jeremiah's personal identity was known to the Lord prior to the moment when Jeremiah was conceived. The God of the Bible is omniscient, and He is the only life giver, so what He says here to Jeremiah in particular can be extended in general to all humans at all times in all places. God knows us before our parents conceive us. Biblically speaking, this is strong evidence that God regards the child in the womb as a human life. Moreover, God's intimate knowledge of the unborn suggests that each life is carefully prepared to fulfill a specific purpose in God's plan for His creation.

At the biological level, note that God also tells Jeremiah, "I formed you in the womb" (Jer. 1:5). This indicates that the development of the child in the womb is the work of God. With the Bible teaching that God "upholds the universe by the word of his power" (Heb. 1:3 ESV), we can also extend what the Lord says in Jeremiah 1:5 to all humans. God sustains the universe, and He is at work in the development of every child in every womb.

If God knows people prior to their being formed in the womb, and if God is the one who forms them in the womb, then surely we are dealing with human beings made in God's image in the womb. So it is not a stretch for us to affirm that the lives of unborn children are equally precious in God's sight. As image bearers, these little ones are endowed—in utero—with the full measure of dignity afforded to all human beings.

What we learn from Jeremiah 1:5 can also be found in Psalm 139. David asserts,

> For it was You who created my inward parts; You
> knit me together in my mother's womb. I will praise
> You because I have been remarkably and wonderfully
> made. . . . My bones were not hidden from You when
> I was made in secret, when I was formed in the depths
> of the earth. Your eyes saw me when I was formless;
> all my days were written in your book and planned
> before a single one of them began. (vv. 13–16)

We see a number of truths about the unborn from this passage. Once again, the passage affirms that God has a personal knowledge of every individual human being prior to their development in the womb. We see this from David's assertion in Psalm 139:16 that all his days were written in God's book when none of them had yet come to be, when his substance was yet unformed. This means that God knew David before he was conceived. Second, we see again that God is at work in the formation of children in the womb: David speaks of God knitting him together in his mother's womb in 139:13, of himself being "made" in 139:14, and of God weaving him together in 139:15 (ESV). Third, David says in 139:15 that his bones, or his frame (ESV), were not hidden from God when he was being made. This means that God was watching over David while he was in the womb. It further testifies to God's active involvement in creating every human life and indicates that we should in fact recognize the personhood of the unborn child.

These passages tell us that God has a personal, comprehensive knowledge of people prior to their conception, that the formation of a human being in the mother's womb is the work of God, and that God oversees the development of babies in the wombs of their mothers. And from these things we gain invaluable perspective on the beauty and sanctity of human life.

Abortion is a savage, brutal, unjust interruption of God's work of bringing about life. As God is working to create that child in the womb, abortion circumvents this good work. In the place of new life, abortion introduces death.

Consider this reality in light of Luke 1:39–44. This description of the unborn John the Baptist's reaction to the coming of Mary, the mother of Jesus, to visit Elizabeth the mother of the Baptist, shows the baby in the womb is capable of joy. Luke relates that "when Elizabeth heard Mary's greeting, the baby leaped inside her" (Luke 1:41), and that Elizabeth then told Mary, "When the sound of your greeting reached my ears, the baby leaped for joy inside me!" (1:44). This passage presents the unborn Baptist rejoicing over Mary the mother of Jesus.

We have known for some time that babies in the womb feel pain. Luke 1:41 indicates that babies in the womb can also feel joy. This too indicates personhood. It is beyond disheartening then that abortion ends any joy that a child might feel in a ripping cut of searing pain.

Having looked at some specific statements the Bible makes about the unborn, these need to be set in the wider biblical context.

God Is for His Image Bearers

In the big story the Bible tells, God made man and woman in His image, blessed them, and the first thing He told them to do was to be fruitful and multiply and fill the earth so that they could subdue it and exercise dominion over all animals (Gen. 1:26–28).

Why would God want the earth to be full of His image bearers? An image is a reflection of the one it represents.[1] To be made in the image and likeness of God is to be a visible representative of the invisible God. The Lord made human beings so that in their subduing the earth and exercising dominion of the world they would make His invisible character visible in all creation.

God wants the world to be filled with people because from the rising of the sun to the place of its setting, God wants His character to be seen. God wants the world to be filled with His glory like the waters fill the seas, so He made man and woman in His image and told them to be fruitful and multiply and fill the earth.[2] Recognizing that mankind bears the image of God is important because of what it represents. Again, because of the image, we believe that every human possesses intrinsic dignity and value. We believe that man is valuable because God is valuable. God receives glory as we reflect His image.

To keep a baby from being born is to rob God of the glory He deserves from that child.

Genesis 2 describes the way God placed the first man and woman in a pristine garden and gave them one prohibition. They were warned not to eat of the fruit of the tree of the knowledge of good and evil, and they were told that if they transgressed and ate the fruit of that tree they would surely die (Gen. 2:17). They ate, and their immediate actions show evidence of spiritual death. They hide from each other, then they hide from God and refuse to answer His questions, shifting the blame away from themselves (Gen. 3:1–13).

God tells the serpent that he will have ongoing conflict with the woman and her seed, and that the seed of the woman will bruise his head (Gen. 3:15). As the man and woman hear what the Lord tells the serpent, they learn that their lives will continue, though eventually they will face physical death (3:19). However, in Genesis 3:15, God has promised that their descendant will overcome the one who introduced evil into His good world. This message of redemption is critical for the future of God's image bearers. Even though sin was introduced at the fall of man, we place our hope in God's promise of a restored humanity that comes through faith in Jesus Christ—the descendant who overcomes evil, crushes the head of the serpent, and restores all that has been lost or distorted because of our rebellion.

But don't miss how this happens. At the most fundamental level, salvation will happen because God will mercifully allow the man and woman to have a child. This means that the whole story of redemption hinges on the birth of a baby. Adam's response to what God says—naming the woman "the mother of all living" (Gen. 3:20)—is an act of faith in response to God's declaration.

God promised redemption when He promised a baby: that the seed of the woman would bruise the serpent's head (Gen. 3:15). Reflecting on this passage, David poetically characterized the way God saves His people in Psalm 8:2, "Because of Your adversaries, You have established a stronghold from the mouths of children and nursing infants to silence the enemy and the avenger." The great enemy of God, David says, will be overcome because a baby will be born. This is how God works. He chooses the weak and helpless things of the world to slay the dragon.

God answered Satan's roar of triumph at his successful temptation of Adam and Eve with the promise of a baby's cry. Then the babe in question was born in Bethlehem, even as the seed of the serpent was trying to have the babies of that city slain. God protected Jesus, and Jesus saved God's children.

The satanic attempt to devour the baby Jesus is dramatized in Revelation 12, where John depicts the ancient dragon, who is the devil and Satan, crouched to spring on the newborn babe when His mother brings him forth. The child is Jesus, the seed of the woman, the one who will rule the nations with a rod of iron (Rev. 12:5). Satan's attempt to devour the child as soon as He is born is thwarted, however, and redemption results. Salvation happened because the baby was born.

From what we see across the Bible's story, we can make the following two assertions:

1. The God of the Bible is the champion of children.
2. Every attempt to kill a baby is fundamentally satanic.

Conclusion

Because the baby Jesus was born, the Bible teaches that the injustice of abortion will not prevail. There will come a day when the slaughter is stopped. Because the baby Jesus was born, there is hope for every woman who has ended the life of her unborn child, hope for every man who pressured a woman to do so, hope for every medical worker engaged in the grand satanic enterprise of putting the babies to death. The blood of Jesus makes forgiveness possible for those who have shed blood. The resurrection of Jesus makes a new life possible for all who regret what they have done.

Jesus will come, and as King He will reign. Every wicked execution of an innocent child will receive just recompense.

Righteousness will be established. Justice will be exalted. Those who repent and trust Christ will be shown mercy. Those who continue in rebellion will face the Risen One in His wrath.

Discussion Questions

1. Why is it inaccurate to say that the Bible is silent on the subject of abortion? Why is it important to affirm the applicability of the Bible's teaching on every ethical question people face?

2. Advocates of abortion appeal to emotional realities such as compassion to justify what the Bible condemns. How can we counteract this and reclaim emotion realities such as love, compassion, and justice? Why is it always wrong to respond to something wicked (such as rape or incest) with more wickedness (abortion)?

3. How does the Bible's inner logic condemn abortion? How is this congruent with support for capital punishment? How should the great value the Bible places on life inform a Christian's response?

4. When does life begin? What evidence can be presented on theological and biblical grounds that life begins at conception? How does the notion of "image of God" inform our understanding on this?

5. The whole story of redemption hinges on the birth of a child. How does the grand scheme of biblical theology inform a holistic pro-life ethic?

CHAPTER

2

What Does the Gospel Say?

Matt Chandler

I HAVE THREE CHILDREN, AND FOR SEVEN OR EIGHT YEARS, they incessantly hounded me about getting pets. My response was always the same: "I have pets." I already had a mammal that went to the bathroom on the floor. I was not looking for another one. I didn't feel any need to add to my family's forces of destruction. But daughters have a weird power over dads, so we got a dog. His name is Gus. He's an Australian Shepherd, and I like him. I don't love him; I like him.

He's a really smart dog, smarter than some of the people I know. I can say, "Go get Audrey up," and he will. He'll pick the right kid, lick her face, pull her covers, and bother her until she gets up—a parent's best friend. All while I'm sipping my coffee at the table. He's a great dog.

Then, God help me, we got a horse, and my oldest daughter named her Gypsy. Within one year I introduced a horse and a dog, which both take time and money, into our family unit.

One morning, on a particularly beautiful day, we went out to the barn where we keep Gypsy, the whole family in tow. I don't like to ride horses, but I think horses are unbelievable. They're just majestic. As I helped Audrey groom her horse that day, I could see Gypsy's muscles clearly. She was just a three-year-old mare, but she was powerful. As I brushed Gypsy, I thought about God's response to Job and how God mentions the horse in particular, describing how majestic it is and how, when a horse really snorts or paws the ground, it can strike terror into the hearts of men. If she'd wanted to, Gypsy could have decided she didn't want me brushing her anymore and could have easily hurt me.

So here I am with a horse and a dog—a very smart dog and a very great horse. The dog is awesome. The horse is incredible. But neither is equal to, or on par with, any human being alive.

Humans are not equal with the rest of the creative order. God has given us a moral, intellectual, spiritual compass that the rest of creation does not possess. This does not give us the right to be brutal or cruel, but God gave man alone dominion over creation.

In Genesis 1:26–27, the Bible says: "Then God said, 'Let Us make man in Our image, according to Our likeness. They will rule the fish of the sea, the birds of the sky, the livestock, all the earth, and the creatures that crawl on the earth.' So God created man in His own image; He created him in the image of God; He created them male and female." This is called the *imago Dei*—humans are unique because we have been made in the image of God.

Humans wrestle with some things that no other created thing does. For example: If you're watching the National Geographic Channel and they show a little baby antelope, you think, *Oh my gosh! That's so cute.* Then three minutes later, there's a female lion ripping it to pieces. You're kind of like, *Oh, I can't . . . ! I just can't . . . ! Oh my gosh!* Right?

Do you know who is not thinking that? The lion.

The lion is not thinking, *I shouldn't be doing this!* There's no moral quandary in the lion. Later that evening, as she's licking the blood off her paws, she's not filled with regret and shame. She isn't thinking, *I did it again! I need some help!* She is driven by instinct alone. She is not wondering about her future. She is not sitting and contemplating what will happen when she is too old to hunt. She is a lion. She is magnificent, but she has no moral or spiritual compass.

But people do. We lie in bed at night with regrets. We wrestle with what is right and what is wrong, or whether we should or shouldn't do something. The animal kingdom doesn't wrestle with those things. Mankind alone has dominion because mankind alone has been made in the image of God.

When it comes to the topic of abortion, then, the first question we have to answer is this: "When does this *imago Dei*—the soul, this moral, spiritual compass—enter into the man or the woman?" That's a huge question. The Bible tells us in Genesis 5:3 that the image is passed from a father to his sons and daughters. So when men have children, they are giving birth to little image bearers—men and women, little boys and little girls. What we see in the Bible is that this moral/spiritual compass—this soul—has a presence in the womb. In Psalm 58:3 (ESV), the Bible says, "The wicked are estranged from the womb; they go astray from birth, speaking lies."

That's a strange text, isn't it? Why bring up wickedness right now? Because the Bible says wickedness, which is a moral state of being, is in place in the womb. Wickedness isn't something that occurs in our hearts after we're born. The soul—that moral, spiritual thing that exists in mankind that sets us beyond the rest of creation—is present in utero.

Job 14:4 says, "Who can produce something pure from what is impure? No one!" This isn't math where a negative multiplied by a negative equals a positive. If dad is a sinner and mom is a sinner, then guess what they have? Sinners.

Job's point is that two unclean things can't possibly produce something that's clean. The argument in Job is the same one we see in Psalms, that the soul is present in the womb. From there Job 15:14 says, "What is man, that he should be pure? Or one born of woman, that he should be righteous?" This is the same argument. The soul is intact in utero.

So now the question is, When, in the womb, does the soul become present? When does life begin? This has implications for a hundred different things in our lives.

Psalm 51:5 says, "Indeed, I was guilty when I was born; I was sinful when my mother conceived me." According to the Word of God, the soul comes into human cellular matter at conception— not after the first trimester or the second trimester. A human being is born, soul intact. When sperm and egg meet and unite, there is a living human being.

This has all sorts of implications. First of all, we should marvel at God's detailed work in creating life. Psalm 139 says He knits us together in our mothers' wombs. It says we are fearfully and wonderfully made. It says God knew all the days we would have before we lived even one of them. In fact, the weight of this text actually points toward God preparing us, while we are in our mothers' wombs, for the things He has planned for us. It's a beautiful text.

Second, as believers in Christ, we should put a high value on all human life. And third, this has massive implications for how we view social issues, none so paramount as the social issue of abortion.

The Worldview behind Abortion

Though this issue is often fought over in the political arena, it is not first and foremost a political issue. This is a biblical, ethical, and spiritual issue by which, to our shame, few of us have been moved.

Because I'm a pastor, I get to have a lot of conversations with people who don't believe in Jesus.

When I sit across from unbelievers and discuss this topic, they will often bring up some kind of scientific data to prove their point. Yet, I'm becoming more and more convinced that what we're dealing with here is not based in logic or reason at all. Repeatedly, I've witnessed the actual science of the matter fall on deaf ears as I speak to those who are secular.

When *Roe v. Wade* was handed down in 1973, there was no 3D ultrasound.[3] We didn't have the ability to watch our babies smile at us before they were born.

But we do know that, at 4 to 6 weeks, the heart typically beats about 113 times per minute. The heart changes color as blood enters and leaves its chambers with each beat. The heart will beat approximately 54 million times before birth.[4]

By 7 weeks hiccups have been observed, along with leg movements and a startle response.[5] The hands can now come together, fingers are separate, toes are joined only at the bases, and knee joints are also present.[6] By 7 1/2 weeks, the pigmented retina of the eye is easily seen, and the eyelids are beginning a period of rapid growth.[7]

Even more alarming is the fact that on May 23, 2013, Public Policy Fellow and professor of neurobiology and anatomy, Maureen L. Condic, presented scientific evidence concerning the ability of unborn children to experience pain at a US House subcommittee.

"To experience pain, a noxious stimulus must be detected. The neural structures necessary to detect noxious stimuli are in place by 8 to 10 weeks of human development. . . . There is universal agreement that pain is detected by the fetus in the first trimester. The debate concerns how pain is experienced; i.e., whether a fetus has the same pain experience a newborn or an adult would have."[8]

By 10 weeks, all of the baby's organs are developing and some of the vital organs—such as kidneys, intestines, brain, and liver—are starting to function.[9] This means that a nervous system has developed, and the brain can receive pain signals. By 11 weeks, the baby is almost fully formed. The bones are beginning to harden, and genitalia are developing externally. By 12 weeks, you can hear your baby's heartbeat at a prenatal checkup. Your baby's just over 2 inches long and weighs about half an ounce.[10] By 22 weeks, a baby, with a little bit of help, can live outside the womb.[11]

Incidence of Abortion in the United States

- Half of the pregnancies among American women are unintended, and 4 in 10 of these are terminated by abortion.
- Twenty-one percent of all pregnancies (excluding miscarriages) end in abortion.
- In 2011, 1.06 million abortions were performed, down 13 percent from 1.21 million in 2008. From 1973 through 2011, nearly 53 million legal abortions occurred.
- Each year, 1.7 percent of women aged fifteen to forty-four have an abortion. Half have had at least one previous abortion.
- At least half of American women will experience an unintended pregnancy by age forty-five, and at 2008 abortion rates, one in ten women will have an abortion by age twenty, one in four by age thirty and three in ten by age forty-five.[12]

Statistically speaking, the overwhelming majority of abortions are not taking place because the mother's life is in danger or even because of rape. Most often, it is purely about convenience.

"I don't want to do it."

"I'm not ready for this."

"I didn't ask for this."

Sadly, what we get is murder for the sake of convenience.

And what ends up happening is that those who support abortion are forced, because they can't argue with the science, to show their cards. And their "pro-choice" views aren't driven by reason at all. Pro-choice advocate Mary Elizabeth Williams wrote an article in *Salon* on January 23, 2013, that illustrates how insane things have become.[13]

She writes, "Yet I know that throughout my own pregnancies, I never wavered for a moment in the belief that I was carrying a human life inside of me. I believe that's what a fetus is: a human life. And that doesn't make me one iota less solidly pro-choice." Think about how crazy that statement is. That, despite having no doubt as to the life being human, Mary still believes it's the woman's right to choose whether or not to terminate that life.

She continues, "Here's the complicated reality in which we live. All life is not equal. That's a difficult thing for liberals like me to talk about, lest we wind up looking like death-panel-loving, kill-your-grandma-and-your-precious-baby storm troopers. Yet a fetus can be a human life without having the same rights as the woman in whose body it resides. She's the boss. Her life and what is right for her circumstances and her health should automatically trump the rights of the non-autonomous entity inside of her. Always."

That's insane! Who chooses whose life has the most value? Who gets that power? That sounds like Nazi Germany to me. That sounds like the Three-Fifths Compromise, when African Americans supposedly comprised three-fifths of a man. Who decides this? To whom do we give this power?

Some abortion advocates respond with, "Well, it's the woman's body." The baby might be in the woman's body, but the baby is not the woman's body. It has its own DNA.[14] It has its own genetic code, its own blood type, its own functioning brain, kidneys, and lungs. The baby is not the woman's body. The baby is *in* the woman's body, but that's not the same thing. And it's not the same because this line of reasoning denies something that is fundamental to our society, the idea of natural rights.

I'm sure you are hearing echoes of the preamble to the Declaration of Independence: "We hold these truths to be self-evident, that all men are created equal, that they are endowed by their Creator with certain unalienable Rights, that among these are Life, Liberty, and the pursuit of Happiness." The right to life is a natural right. It doesn't say we are born with natural rights but that we are created with them.

So when people argue for abortion because a woman should have complete freedom to choose what she does with her own body, that's just not true. Sure, we live in a "free country" where all manner of privileges are granted to us as citizens, like voting or driving or drawing Social Security.[15] But those are "conferred rights"—privileges extended to citizens by the government. The government absolutely has the right to prohibit you from prostituting yourself or driving 95 mph on the interstate, and it certainly has the obligation to protect the natural rights of every person.

But my point is that a baby in a mother's womb is a person who is endowed with, and should be protected by, natural rights. This kind of weird, ethereal pro-choice rhetoric that seeks to reduce abortion to a conversation about a woman's body is so detached from rational thought. It shows our consciences have been seared. People oppose laws that would protect the unborn on the grounds of not wanting the government to tell them what they can do with their bodies. But our government gets to tell us all sorts of things we can and can't do. Right now it's telling us we can murder babies. That is tragic. As Christians, we need to be the ones making the argument that someone's inclination to abort should never trump another person's natural rights. There is nothing more fundamental or important than the right to life.

Nothing More Powerful than the Gospel

One of the things I love about the Word of God is this: God pulls from the fringes of darkness His brightest lights. Saul of Tarsus kicked doors open in Corinth and dragged women and men out into the street, binding them and killing them. He persecuted Christians. David, a man after God's own heart, committed adultery with a woman and then had her husband murdered. Moses killed a man with his bare hands.

There is no sin with more power than the gospel of Jesus Christ, not even abortion. If abortion had more power than the gospel, we wouldn't be talking about it. If it were able to define a person, we wouldn't be talking about it. Christ's forgiveness defines us. Newness of life is made available to all who repent and seek His face.

Every time I've preached on the subject of abortion, I use Ephesians 5:11. "Don't participate in the fruitless works of darkness, but instead expose them."

It seems like it will only be a matter of time until *Roe v. Wade* will be overturned because the science is on our side. With that said, God has almost always accomplished social change through the outcry of His people who are against the world for the sake of the world. There are these defining moments of history that we wish we could have experienced. We wish we could have fought alongside those who cried out.

I look at my own bloodline, my own family. Where were they when Jim Crow was happening? What were they doing? When the oppression and injustice that rested so heavily on African Americans in this country, particularly in the South, was occurring, what was my family doing? I don't quite know the answer to that question. I do know that there's no one in my family who marched with Dr. King.

I'm convinced that forty years from now, our grandbabies are going to think we were barbaric. They're going to wonder what we were doing and how we just sat by and did nothing. Did we just sit on the sidelines and refuse to engage?

The Gospel and Abortion: How Do We Engage?

First, we must repent of our indifference. In reality, there's not much difference between Mary Elizabeth Williams, whom I quoted above, and us. So many people say, "Yeah, abortion ends life. I'm not doing it. That's how I'm taking my stand: I'm not going to do it." We need to repent of being indifferent. We just haven't cared. We haven't done anything.

Second, we need to pray. We need to pray because it is painfully obvious that this argument is no longer rational. More than anything else, I think this is now a spiritual issue. We really are dealing with a seared conscience, and the arguments are no longer based in reason.

For instance, all fifty states in the US have strict laws protecting animals from human beings.[16] If you kill a puppy, then you go to jail. Kill a baby, and you're fine. Yet thirty-eight states have fetal homicide laws, and at least twenty-three states have fetal homicide laws that apply to the earliest stages of pregnancy ("any state of gestation," "conception," "fertilization," or "post-fertilization").[17] If a pregnant woman gets in her car to drive to the abortion clinic and, while driving there, a drunk driver hits the car and kills her baby, that driver gets charged with homicide. They get arrested, prosecuted, and sentenced to jail. But if she makes it to the abortion clinic, a doctor can—for a fee—take a vacuum pump and suck a baby, with a brain and nerve endings, out of the womb in pieces. That's a seared conscience. That's madness. That's the type of argument that's no longer rooted in any type of thoughtfulness. Yes, we're going to need to pray. Pray and pray and pray and pray and pray.

In Daniel, chapter 9, Daniel confessed the sins of the nation of Israel. They weren't necessarily his sins but the sins of the nation of Israel. He pled with God to be merciful, to intervene, to straighten out their path, to call them back to their priests and the Law and to call them back to the way of God. We need to pray that way.

Third, we must learn that our faith must inform how we vote. Please, let me be clear: Abortion is bigger than any one political party. But our faith should inform how we vote. I'm not talking Republican or Democrat—I'm not talking about that. But I am saying that our faith must bear weight on our decision-making.

Some who are more politically informed might be thinking, *I can't believe you, Chandler. You're a one-issue voter?* Everyone is a one-issue voter. There are thousands of "one-issues" people rally around. However, you can be pro-life and also be a high-functioning moron who has no business in public office. There are some guys who are very pro-life whom I would rather not elect to run anything. There are pro-life guys I wouldn't trust with my wallet. A candidate having "pro-life" beside his or her name on a yard sign doesn't guarantee my support.

Fourth, we must get off the sideline and get involved. This is not a popular position to take. Standing for life will not make you seem enlightened to your peers. Numerically, I will not grow my church by preaching about this, which is a small price to pay for rallying God's people toward what is true and right and good before the King of Glory.

We must get involved. Involvement isn't all you think it is. When all's said and done, involvement must not shake its fist at the darkness, but be like light in darkness. To call abortion murder is calling it what it is, but it doesn't fix the problem. The church and its people must become a beacon of hope and light for women in difficult circumstances.

Conclusion

Not long ago, after finishing a sermon at my church, I met a young woman named Sarah. She had the tags we give to parents when they check their children into our kids' ministry, so I knew she was a mom. Sarah told me that she lived with some other young women, including her sister, in a house in Denton, Texas. She had a drug issue, and she was stripping to pay the bills. She had her kids taken away from her and had also been evicted from her house. But some young women from our church had been praying for her and had let her move in with them. Then they brought Sarah to The Village. She said of her first weekend, "God was here. God was here!"

Sarah found out she was pregnant and decided to go to the abortion clinic. But the young women she was living with said, "Don't do this. There are other ways. We can figure it out."

But Sarah was determined, so she got in her car and drove to the clinic.

The women she was living with began to pray. Sarah went to the abortion clinic and, a couple of hours later, came home. She told the women, "Well, it looks like this baby is living. God was at the abortion clinic." These women rallied around Sarah, loved her, encouraged her, and were there for her. And a member from our church is adopting the baby Sarah is carrying.

This is how we get involved. It's not by shaking our fists at the darkness or by merely voting a certain way. That doesn't work. The reason young ministers avoid this topic altogether is that they don't understand how to lovingly engage as they speak the truth about abortion and human dignity. The church should be a community marked by our love for women and our support of women. We must be willing to open our homes, open up our checkbooks, and open up space and time in our lives—all for the glory of God, the salvation of others, and the protection of life.

Years from now, when my grandchildren ask, "Hey, Pops, this seems like it was so barbaric. What in the world was going on?" I want to be able to say, "We fought our guts out. In fact, the reason you know it's barbaric is because a great number of people sacrificed and labored and didn't quit." This has to become our heartbeat. This has to be consistent. It has to be "what we do" moving forward.

We must pay more attention to the way we spend money so we can free up more money to support adoption. We must foster an adoption culture. We must create space in our homes where people who have fallen on difficult times can join us for a season and be loved back to health. This is Christian hospitality. The alternative is to cross our fingers and hope for change while another million babies are murdered.

Who is going to carry their flag? Who is going to stand in their defense? When we talk about the Civil Rights Movement, we talk about Martin Luther King Jr. Why? Because he was the voice. He was the flag. He was the one saying, "Not on our watch!"

The unborn can't do it. The unborn don't have one among them who might lead or protect them. That responsibility falls on us. The Bible clearly says our call is to the least of these. Who is more "least" than the unborn? There is no genocide or war subjecting people to the kind of oppression, violence, and unjust slaughter than there is in the murder of the unborn.

God help us.

Discussion Questions

1. How does the *imago Dei* inform the way Christians think about abortion? Why does our faith demand that we act to protect the unborn?

2. What would you say to a friend who defends abortion even while acknowledging that a human life is at stake? As a Christian, how can you advocate for truth in the midst of a culture of death?

3. In what ways are Christians in your community actively engaged in pro-life ministry? How could you be personally involved in protecting the unborn?

4. For many Americans, abortion is understood in categories of either political "right" or political "left." Why is it important for Christians to show that fundamentally protecting human life is actually one of moral right and wrong? How can this case be made from Scripture?

5. How should the issue of life affect your political and cultural engagement?

3

How Should the Christian Live?

Karen Swallow Prior

LIKE NO OTHER ISSUE TODAY, THE CONFLICT OVER ABORTION requires us to wrestle with all that it means to be human. To consider abortion is to reckon with profound ontological, theological, and sociological questions. What is a human being? How do we handle responsibly the procreative power of sexuality? And how do we balance the rights of individuals as moral agents having a free will with the rights of those dependent upon them and the society in which we exist together? If we could agree upon answers to these questions, the abortion issue would be easily solved.

In addition to being a challenging human question, the abortion issue poses particular challenges to the Christian living in a world in which abortion is almost a given. The abortion issue poses complex questions for the Christian living in a post-Christian culture. What does it mean to be made in the image of God, even in a society that no longer believes we are? Is banning abortion an attempt to impose biblical morality on others or is it advancing social good? How do we apply and balance the biblical principles of truth and love, justice and mercy, in the context of abortion? We can be confident that even if the answers to these great questions cannot be agreed upon, we can still press forward in the truth that no one can really deny: abortion deeply wounds individuals, families, and society.

The entirety of the whole human drama is captured in the abortion debate: the tragedy and the comedy. In fact, the traditional symbol of drama—the weeping face that represents tragedy and the laughing face that represents comedy—provides an apt symbol for the issue. As pro-life Christians, we acknowledge the weeping caused by abortion at the same time we offer the possibility of joy. As Christians, it is not enough to say no to death. We must also say yes to life. We must not be just *against abortion* but truly *for life*.

History: The Tragedy of Abortion
vs. the Comedy of Life

It is easy in the midst of whatever current cultural climate we find ourselves in to be shortsighted and—consequently, in the case of something that has as strong a grip on our culture as abortion does—to despair. Thus, understanding the current state of the abortion debate from within the longer perspective of history, and even more, from the perspective of God's Word, as well and church history is crucial. We cannot, therefore, think of abortion as primarily a political issue or one that can be resolved by mere proclamations or pronouncements. We must, rather, challenge abortion according to all the complexities raised in a culture in which it has become so deeply rooted.

We have not always had such wide-scale, unfettered abortion as we have in America today. Abortion as we now know it—rampant, legalized abortion-on-demand—has existed for just two generations. It was only in the twentieth century that abortion came to be seen not only as a right, but even a thing to be celebrated as an advance for women's freedom and independence. Our wide-scale acceptance of abortion is an aberration in human history, and a recent one at that.

Even among feminists, abortion has not long been considered a means of progress for women. The "first wave" feminists of the late nineteenth and early twentieth centuries, including suffragists such as Susan B. Anthony, Victoria Woodhull, and Elizabeth Cady Stanton, opposed abortion. Early advocates for women's equality recognized abortion as a harm to women as well as children and viewed it as evidence of society's failure to meet the needs of women and their families. Abortion was never necessary for women's rights. It became necessary only within the context of the sexual revolution.

While abortions in modern America number millions upon millions (nearly 60 million since 1973), it's important to consider abortion within the perspective of human history. Even before its widespread acceptance, abortion has always existed. In reviewing the history of abortion, two important insights emerge: first, for most of history, abortion was not viewed differently from killing or exposing born infants, and second, the prerogative of fathers in ancient cultures to accept or reject a child foreshadows the same right given to mothers in modern Western cultures today.

Records from both history and literature offer evidence for how acceptable the killing of children was in ancient times. Some of the world's great myths and stories center on the attempted killing of an infant or child. The tragic hero of the famous Oedipus myth was rescued as an infant after being pierced through the feet and left to die at the order of his father, the king. The legend of the founding of Rome is based on twin boys, Romulus and Romus, who were put in the Tiber River as infants to die. And even the fairy tale of Snow White centers on the failed attempt to have the child killed. Of course, stories reflect values, not facts, but even in this way, such tales are illuminating.

The facts, however, are even more horrific. The early church father Tertullian attests to the pagan practices of "choosing some of the cruelest [deaths] for their own children, such as drowning, or starving with cold or hunger, or exposing to the mercy of dogs, dying by the sword being too sweet a death for children . . ."[18] Various modern discoveries confirm the truth of Tertullian's charge. In 2014, for example, an archaeologist discovered the skeletal remains of more than 100 infants experts say were killed within a week of their births. Numerous similar discoveries have been made over the years.[19] The killing of newborns was considered a form of birth control and such infants were not viewed as fully human.

In patriarchal cultures, wives and children were considered the property of the husband, so abortion was generally viewed as an offense against a husband, as destruction of his property. For example, ancient Assyrian law considered a wife and her children to be the property of her husband, and a woman who procured an abortion was to be put to death, "impaled and not buried."[20] Both Plato and Aristotle recommended abortion and infanticide, without distinguishing between offspring in the womb or out, as ways to limit family size in service to the needs of society. While the Hippocratic Oath of the fourth century BC prohibited the administration of abortion by a physician, some scholars think the objection was out of concern for the life and health of the mother, not the unborn child.[21]

Some of the most significant testimony of the ancient practices of child killing (both inside and outside the womb) comes from accounts in the Bible and from the early church. The many references to child killing by the church fathers indicate just how widely accepted these practices were in the ancient Greco-Roman world.

The Bible does not really distinguish between the infant in the womb or the one out of it. The willful destruction of unborn children appears in the Bible only in accounts of cultures at war with God's people (see, for example, 2 Kings 15:16). To lose a child in the womb—whether accidentally or through warfare— is presented in the Bible as a loss, a curse, a harm, and a tragedy. The prophet Jeremiah, for example, describes in chapter 31 the inconsolable weeping of Rachel over the loss of her children. Yet, in that same chapter, Jeremiah gives the promise of the Lord to replace the sorrow of His people with comfort and joy. God's promise is that even in so great a tragedy as the loss of a child, He will remove our mask of tears, and let us wear the face of laughter.

Because of the need to resist assimilation into the surrounding pagan culture, the early church provides a thorough record of opposition to the practices of abortion and infanticide. In his book *Third Time Around: A History of the Pro-Life Movement*

from the First Century to the Present, George Grant documents
the early church's sustained chorus against abortion. The apos-
tolic teachings found in the first-century *Didache* includes the
admonition, "There are two ways: the way of life and the way of
death . . . Therefore, do not murder a child by abortion or kill a
newborn infant." Similarly, a second-century church tract stated,
"You shall not slay a child by abortion. You shall not kill that
which has already been generated." A second-century Christian
apologist, Athenagoras, wrote, "The fetus in the womb is a living being and therefore the object of God's care." Clement of
Alexandria stated unequivocally that abortion is "outright murder of the fetus" and Ambrose cautioned that those who take
abortifacient drugs "snuff out the life in their womb." Jerome
called abortion "the murder of an unborn child." And Augustine
condemned the "poisonous drugs" that "murder the unborn
child."[22]

The early church did more than just condemn abortion,
however. The church fathers offered important theological and
ontological insights into the status of unborn life. While many
throughout history and today would like to believe that the soul
enters the body at some later point in pregnancy (or even birth),
Gregory of Nyssa insisted that the soul and body cannot exist
apart from one another, stating, "there is but one beginning
of both" and that is at the point of "generation" (or conception).[23] While views within the early church about the point of

ensoulment differed, the church fathers agreed with Tertullian's view that "there is no difference whether you destroy a child in its formation, or after it is formed and delivered."[24]

In contrast to the surrounding cultures, the Bible does not speak directly of intentional abortion. It's as though such a thing is unimaginable in God's Kingdom. Instead, the Bible is filled with joyful images attesting to the humanity of children born and unborn. Children are described uniformly and unequivocally throughout the Bible as blessings.

One of the most cited passages about nascent children is Psalm 139, which describes how each person is knit together by God in the womb. Ecclesiastes 11:5 (ESV) tells us that the "spirit comes to the bones in the womb." Samson's mother was told that her son would be set apart "to God from the womb" (Judg. 13:5 ESV). The psalmist declares that "You have been my God from my mother's womb" (22:10). The prophets Isaiah and Jeremiah both state that God called them from the womb (Isa. 49:1; Jer. 1:5). And the unborn baby of Zechariah leaped in his mother's womb at the arrival of Mary who was carrying Jesus inside (Luke 1:41–44).

As is seen from both the Bible and history, laws and mores around abortion reflect a society's values and priorities. The acceptance of abortion and infanticide in ancient cultures was rooted in a patriarchal system that prioritized a man's property rights—which included his wife and children—over human life itself. In ancient cultures the father as provider of the family unit had governance over the entire family, a custom called *paterfamilias*. The legalization of abortion in America, in the name of sexual freedom and individual autonomy, replaced the absolute right of the fathers under *paterfamilias* with the absolute right of the mother over the child. Today, the mother, as provider of the body in which the unborn child temporarily lives and moves and has his/her being, has been given similar right. But the right to life is a human right, one that comes from God and must take precedence over all other human rights since without life, no other rights matter.

The Current Scene

In issuing its *Roe v. Wade* decision, the US Supreme Court declared that the judicial body "need not resolve the difficult question of when life begins."[25] So instead, *Roe v. Wade* made abortion legal for any reason in the first and second trimester, and legal for the life or health of the mother in the third trimester. In a lesser-known companion ruling handed down on the same day, *Doe v. Bolton*,[26] the court defined "health" so broadly that it could include virtually anything that might have a negative impact on a pregnant woman. The Supreme Court's rulings on abortion were radical by any measure. In fact, many pro-choice legal scholars and abortion rights supporters fault the legal reasoning of the court. Even the pro-choice Supreme Court Justice Ruth Bader Ginsburg has said of the court's decision, "Heavy-handed judicial intervention was difficult to justify and appears to have provoked, not resolved, conflict."[27] Not surprisingly, the extreme position staked out by the court ruling has undergone tempering in the ensuing years.

For example, because the court made abortion legal across the country through the entire pregnancy, a gray area about when exactly birth begins and ends has developed. Some contend that a baby is not born until entirely emerged from the birth canal or even until the umbilical cord is cut. This led to the grisly late-term abortion procedure known as "partial birth abortion," by which the child is killed while still partly in the birth canal which was considered legal since the baby was not technically born. News stories about these abortions, followed by a high profile criminal case in which attempted late-term abortions turned into the murder of newborns, shined the light on just how extreme the law of the land is as a result of *Roe v. Wade*.

Even the very foundation of the ruling is rooted in an extreme view. In basing the right to abortion explicitly on the right to privacy (a right not mentioned in the US Constitution but only inferred), *Roe v. Wade* grounded itself in a modern and radical autonomy that seems on the way toward expending itself. The recent growing unease with unfettered abortion rights might be attributed, at least in part, with the recognition of the limits of extreme individualism. After all, a woman's choice to have an abortion is a decision arrived at through an intricate web of social connections. And her decision reverberates through that network in return. "No man is an island," the seventeenth-century poet and minister John Donne famously wrote. No woman or child is either.

Thus there is growing recognition of the communal aspects of abortion. Currently, men who want to keep and care for an unborn child have no legal say in the abortion decision. Yet, more men who have been involved in an abortion are wrestling with post-abortion guilt and trauma.[28] As they share their stories more and more, ministries designed to meet their needs are emerging.[29] Similarly, the post-Roe generations (those born after 1973) comprise the first population to grow up with a significant percentage of their own siblings having been aborted. With approximately one in four pregnancies ending in abortion (in earlier years, the figure was one in three), this means that countless men and siblings are missing family members right along with the mothers who chose abortion.

Beyond the familial interconnectedness of the abortion decision is the global aspect. In many cultures where boys are valued more than girls, sex-selective abortion is being used to snuff out the lives of unborn girls. This is tragic not only for the unborn girls whose lives are ended but for culture as a whole in perpetuating the devaluing of female lives. Furthermore, social engineering that results in cultures where men far outnumber women has far-reaching implications for the families and social structures of the future.

These ripple effects of abortion that go beyond the pro-choice mantra, "My body, my choice," are making a difference. The hope abortion initially offered of freedom, privacy, and equality is being seen for the false promise it always was. In fact, the percentage of Americans who believe abortion should be legal under all circumstances (which is essentially the current law of the land) rose steadily following *Roe v. Wade*, but peaked in the 1990s and has, for the most part, fallen since then to remain under 30 percent.[30] Furthermore, the rate of abortion following its legalization in 1973 saw a rapid climb to its peak in 1981 of 29.3 abortions per 1,000 women aged fifteen to forty-four. But in recent years, the rate has dropped to 16.9 percent, the lowest rate since legalization.[31]

Along with the human element, technology has surely played a role in lowering acceptance and approval of abortion. Only a generation ago, a child's first baby pictures were taken after birth. Now the technology that allows us to see the child developing in the womb provides photographs from the earliest stages of pregnancy. As a result, an entire generation has grown up with baby albums documenting their lives well before birth, providing a record of individual life in which birth is one step, not the first, along the life journey. It's impossible to measure the role this has on the consistent, if not growing, percentage of Americans identifying as pro-life.

Technology also is making it harder and harder for abortion providers to keep hidden what happens during abortions at every stage. Early in the modern pro-life movement, the late Dr. Bernard Nathanson used ultrasound technology to record a first trimester abortion while it was happening. This resulted in the groundbreaking 1984 video *The Silent Scream*. Nathanson, was an obstetrician who performed countless abortions and helped found the National Association for the Repeal of Abortion Laws (now called NARAL Pro-Choice America) before changing his mind about abortion (and eventually converting to Christianity). His work helped galvanize the pro-life movement of the later twentieth century.

More recently, a different use of technology helped rouse the pro-life movement when hidden cameras were used to expose the disturbing trade in fetal remains by Planned Parenthood, the nation's largest single provider of abortion. Undercover footage capturing officials' callous discussions with prospective buyers about performing procedures so as to obtain the most desired fetal parts (including livers, limbs, heads, and intact cadavers) and the protest that ensued began a movement to defund the organization at state and federal levels.

While abortion remains legal for any reason up until birth, paradoxically, the lives of the unborn are gaining increasing protection apart from abortion in the form of fetal homicide laws. Such laws reflect the growing recognition that the unborn child has a separate life worth legal protection, even if this recognition does not carry over to abortion laws.[32] Thirty-eight states have fetal homicide laws, and at least twenty-eight states have such laws that include unborn children at the earliest stages of pregnancy.[33] Yet, while in many cases other people can be charged for killing an unborn child, the mother still has the right to make that life-or-death decision. Since the life of the unborn child depends entirely upon the will of the mother (just as in ancient times it depended on the will of the father), those who wish to protect the life of the child must do so by influencing, educating, and helping the mother. Accomplishing this requires a multi-pronged effort.

Abortion Law

One prong of such an effort is legislation. The law is a teacher, and as such, helps influence our decisions. Even without overturning *Roe v. Wade*, abortion laws offering some protection reflect both a growing recognition of the humanity of the child in the womb as well as the harm abortion can do to women. Perhaps the least controversial limit on abortion is banning partial-birth abortion. Nineteen states have enacted such bans in recent years. Limiting public funding of abortion is another way to advance a pro-life ethic. Thirty-two states and the District of Columbia limit the use of state funds. Eleven states allow restrictions of abortion coverage of abortion in private insurance plans. Most states allow individual health care providers and institutions to refuse to participate in an abortion. Seventeen states require informed consent, meaning that abortion providers must give women mandated information before the abortion: the possible link between abortion and breast cancer (5 states), the ability of a fetus to feel pain (12 states), or long-term mental health consequences for the woman (7 states). Twenty-eight states have a waiting period between a woman receiving required information about an abortion and having the abortion procedure performed. Thirty-eight states require either parental consent or notification in the case of a minor child getting an abortion. Twenty-one states have laws requiring that abortions done after a certain point in the pregnancy be performed in a hospital. Eighteen require a second physician after a designated time into the pregnancy. Shockingly, not all states require an abortion to be performed by a licensed physician: only thirty-eight have such a requirement.[34] The momentum in passing these kinds of state laws limiting abortion seems to be growing as more state-level restrictions were placed on abortion between 2011 and 2013 than in the previous decade.[35] Since 2011, 230 pro-life laws have been passed.[36] It's important to remember that before *Roe v. Wade*, state laws reigned over abortion. State laws might be a way back. In addition to state laws, the list of legislation considered by Congress continues to grow.[37] One of the earliest and most long-standing federal efforts is the Hyde Amendment, first passed in 1976, banning federal programs from providing health insurance coverage for abortion.

What Should We Do?

It's important as Christians not to put total faith in the political process or in legislation. Our kingdom is not of this world. Yet, if God's providence has placed us in a country that is "of the people, by the people, and for the people," and where (unlike so many of our brothers and sisters throughout the world) being a Christian and standing up for biblical principles is a freedom we are ordained by God to have, then it is our duty to steward well our voices and our votes to advance the common good. Charles Colson offered wisdom on this matter when he rightly cautioned the church to "avoid utopianism and diversion from its transcendent mission," but urged the church, on the other hand, "not to ignore the political scene."[38] Furthermore, even lack of political or legislative success can be successful: evidence indicates that even when proposed laws aren't successfully passed, states often see a decline in abortion rates as result of the awareness raised by public debate.[39]

But changing the laws is not enough. Again, we must not be merely against abortion but must also be supportive of life.

This is the powerful role that crisis pregnancy centers play. These centers are the quiet, sustaining oases in the desert of America's abortion landscape. One recent accounting shows that crisis pregnancy centers far outnumber abortion providers in America at twenty-five hundred and eighteen hundred, respectively.[40] In their earliest days, these centers provided free pregnancy tests and sometimes raised controversy with accusations by abortion providers of trying to frighten women out of abortions. However rudimentary the beginnings of these centers were, they have evolved into some of the most effective and far-reaching local ministries of any kind. Most pregnancy centers now offer a range of services to pregnant and parenting women (and men) that usually include ultrasounds, parenting classes, clothing and furniture, health care, adoption services, and post-abortion counseling. It's estimated that centers around the country serve about one million clients each year.[41] Services are free to clients, and many of the staff members are volunteers. Their services are so expansive that pregnancy centers provide a way for every pro-life Christian and every local congregation to help in concrete ways: answering phones, raising funds, donating items, counseling clients, referring pregnant women in crisis. The stories of the women served by pregnancy centers and the children here today because of them are the best answers to all the complexities that swirl around the politics of the abortion debate.

In addition to helping women make and carry out life-affirming decisions, crisis pregnancy centers also provide support to women who have made the decision to have an abortion. These women who have lived through the agony of abortion are, perhaps, the most powerful witness we have for the lives of the unborn and the pain of abortion. Those who minister to these women—and, increasingly, men who have been involved in abortion—are doing double duty: not only are they helping to restore shattered lives and souls, but since many women who have had one abortion are likely to have repeated abortions, post-abortion ministry can help break the cycle. Countless women have been brought to the Christian faith through post-abortion experiences and offer some of the most powerful pro-life voices today.

Yet, even pro-choice women increasingly attest to abortion's tragic nature. More and more women who have had an abortion and claim not to regret it are stepping forward to describe experiences no one should find acceptable. One cover story in *New York Magazine* featured twenty-six raw, honest accounts of abortion by women who, for the most part, remain pro-choice. Representing a range of ages, socio-economic backgrounds, and circumstances, their stories convey a sense of longing and despair. Not one celebrates abortion as liberating. Instead, the stories shared retell the anguish of an upcoming anniversary of the baby's due date, of being pressured by boyfriends to have the abortions, of ejecting the aborted baby while at home alone, of thinking about how old the baby would be had he or she lived. Organizations like The Abortion Survivor's Network, Priests for Life, and Hope after Abortion are helping women with stories like these overcome the pain and share their stories in order to spare others from the same.

As both statistics and the testimony of women bear out, abortion is pervasive in our culture. But it's not the first time in history this has been so. Furthermore, this deep-rootedness, rather than bringing only despair, offers endless opportunities and ways for each of us to make a difference: by voting for pro-life candidates and laws, by volunteering, educating, giving, praying, and by making our voices heard at opportune times. Christians have every reason to be confidently, boldly, and unapologetically pro-life. We are called to affirm the life of both mother and child, even in the face of difficult circumstances, by offering and modeling joy in embracing life.

Discussion Questions

1. How is being "pro-life" different from being "anti-abortion"?
2. How does knowing abortion's place in history and its treatment by the early church make a difference in how we might approach it today?

3. What are ways in which abortion works against women's freedom and place in society?
4. What are the ways that abortion uniquely impacts men?
5. How can the church make the most impact in challenging abortion in our culture?

How Should the Church Engage?

Charmaine Crouse Yoest

EMMA BECK WAS A YOUNG ENGLISH ARTIST, PREGNANT WITH twins. She was living with Ben, the father of the babies, but he "reacted badly" to the news of her pregnancy, and they broke up. In a sordidly common tale, Emma felt pressured to abort the twins. After canceling her first appointment, she eventually went through with the abortion. She never got over that traumatic decision, and less than a year later, on the eve of her birthday, Emma hung herself.[42]

In the suicide note she left, Emma made it clear that the abortion was a source of unresolvable grief for her,

> *Living is hell for me. I should never have had an abortion* . . . I was frightened, now it is too late. I died when my babies died. I want to be with my babies—they need me, no one else does.

At the inquest, the coroner, Dr. Carlyon concluded: "It is clear that the termination of pregnancy can have a profound effect on a woman's life." This statement does seem self-evidently true. But it is not widely accepted as true by everyone, and in fact is actively contested by abortion proponents.

As we consider how the local church should engage the culture on abortion, it's important to start with what abortion actually is. We can't answer how we engage, until we deeply understand why we as local congregations are called to engage.

Many believers—even the most faithful among us—shy away from the abortion controversy, feeling discomfort with the contentiousness surrounding the discussion, often consigning it to a frame of "politics," which carries with it the whiff of spiritual illegitimacy. Wanting to avoid being "political" and "judgmental," some churches just sidestep the issue entirely, or hermetically seal it inside a box marked "Activism." But leaving the abortion issue to the politically-minded subset within our church who want to organize a bus to attend the annual March for Life, and thereby checking it off the list, misses the imperative to engage holistically and meaningfully with one of the most spiritually significant evils of our day. To treat abortion as a "political issue" ignores the scope of what the life and culture of a local church can do to be salt and light in their community. This mistake is rooted in a fundamental misunderstanding of the reality of abortion.

Despite more than forty years of cultural conflict and conversation, we are still dramatically divided over the ontology of abortion. In fact, perhaps at no other time since the *Roe v. Wade* decision establishing the legality of abortion has the debate over the procedure itself been so focused on its nature and definition. Throughout the '80s and '90s abortion rights advocates centered their arguments on "privacy" and "choice." But as those words grew tired, and with the surge in political power brought by the Obama Administration, abortion advocates changed their tactics and their vernacular and initiated a new campaign: the objective became defining abortion as fundamental health care, no different from any other surgical procedure.

The debate over Obamacare became their preferred vehicle for this shift in language. A quintessential moment came in the summer of 2009 during a debate in the House Education and Labor Committee after Rep. Mark Souder, Indiana Republican, offered an amendment to exclude abortion funding from health care reform. Rep. Lynn Woolsey, California Democrat, clearly miffed, responded,

> [Abortion] is a legal medical practice and by even
> having to talk about it . . . we're not talking about
> having your tonsils out and whether you can or can't.
> It's all based on religious matters and ideas that differ-
> ent people have.[43]

The context of her remarks make it clear that she meant that if we aren't debating whether or not we include a tonsillectomy in health care coverage, neither should we be debating the inclusion of abortion. Clearly, for activists and politicians alike, abortion isn't just a "political" issue. It's an issue worth banking their existence upon. So must it be for how the local church engages.

Buttressing this political strategy was a deliberate cultural shift within the ranks of abortion advocacy leadership: they began to emphasize "owning" the abortion experience. For example, abortion activist, Jennifer Baumgardner, the coauthor of *Abortion and Life* spearheaded an "I Had an Abortion" T-shirt campaign.[44] It was intended, she said, to combat abortion stigma and to tell women "you don't have to be sorry." Then, in the fall of 2014, the President of Planned Parenthood, Cecile Richards, published an article entitled, "Ending the Silence that Fuels Abortion Stigma" in *Elle* magazine acknowledging her own abortion. "I had an abortion," she wrote. "It was the right decision for me and my husband, and it wasn't a difficult decision."[45]

The consistency of the moral equivalency strategy is clear: Abortion isn't difficult. It is common and routine. We aren't debating tonsillectomies; nor should we abortion. Women don't hide appendectomies; nor should they abortion.

The challenge, of course, is Emma Beck. Women don't commit suicide after tonsillectomies and appendectomies—her story more accurately reflects real women and real experience. Abortion is not a tonsillectomy; it is not an appendectomy. It is a real death—of a living human being. The church must fully realize this truth and engage with it because a real death of a living human being has moral weight and spiritual consequence. Christians must own and echo this truth. The church must bear witness to it and offer refuge to those suffering under its weight.

The woman does not choose the consequences. They simply exist. Increased suicide risk. Depression. Anxiety.[46] Something real and significant happens inside an abortion clinic, and the consequences can neither be chosen nor willed away.

At the heart of the abortion advocate's argument for "choice" is the fallacy that the life of the baby is dependent upon the mother's decision for moral weight. According to their narrative, if she chooses life, the baby comes into its own moral standing and has significance—at some indeterminate period of time. Following on their (ill)logic, if she chooses otherwise, chooses the baby's destruction, then it falls into a gray zone of cosmic irrelevancy.

But the baby—with its own beating heart and its own DNA—is an independent variable. Not a dependent one.

Personal Sorrow: The Depth of Loss

My first pregnancy was something of a surprise. But a welcome one. We told everyone almost immediately. And the very next day, the first physical signs of trouble appeared. The doctor told me to stay in bed for a week and then come back to see him. I remember feeling a strange, aching fatigue. I slept and slept, and cried a lot, in an emotional confusion. I had only consciously known of this pregnancy a mere sunrise to sunset. I had not longed for it. But when I returned to the doctor and he told me the baby had not survived, a kind of almost tangible sorrow swept over me. I felt guilty for my sadness; I did not feel I had "earned" it because my actual experience was so brief, benign, and ordinary.

But I could not rationalize my way into setting aside the sorrow quickly. As it turned out, my mourning was not volitional. It was an independent variable, a reality outside my own choice, my own will. Something real had happened. And my body knew it.

I was given space to mourn. My grief was validated by my family and my community. But where does a woman turn when the grief is rooted in abortion, and totally unexpected?

Abortion Ends Life

To spend time reading post-abortion stories is sobering—regardless of whether the compiler has a pro-life or an abortion advocacy perspective, lament seeps through. Even those sad stories gathered to press for the endurance of abortion rights often unintentionally underscore grief and trauma, albeit tinged with defiance and defensiveness.[47] A common theme that emerges is the piercing awareness that something significant has happened following the abortion.

One woman, who posted her story online anonymously when she was sixty years old, recalled getting pregnant and getting an abortion when she was eighteen,

> I woke up so empty. It's an emptiness I can't describe.
> It was so overwhelming. I felt so alone and still do—
> thirty-seven years later.[48]

Another woman, now in her late forties, got an abortion when she was twenty-one and going through a divorce:

> I realized it was my baby the very second I felt my
> baby's soul leaving my body. I remember crying and
> wanting to die because I just killed my baby.[49]

How can women who have entered an abortion facility, set in their decision, almost instantly regret that decision? What changed? We can't understand that reaction, and fully comprehend the reality of abortion, unless we explore that question. Unless we grapple with what abortion actually is: the death of a living human being.

Abortion is not the same as a tonsillectomy. It is not the same as appendicitis. Even in the church we tend to avoid the reality of how abortion is unique: a woman rejecting the life kindled in her body. Even in the church we can sometimes slide into bracketing abortion as a political issue, not as a real death. We must overcome the temptation to sideline or minimize the realities of abortion if we are to faithfully engage. With grace and compassion, we must bear faithful witness to the truth.

Grief Requires Ministry

An unexpected source highlighted the significance of this reality a few years ago. Causing a furor among her feminist friends, the author Naomi Wolf wrote a controversial essay in *The New Republic* in 1995. Her piece entitled, "Our Bodies, Our Souls," wrestled with how feminists approach the spiritual dimension of abortion. She ended up critiquing the still-dominant approach of denying the existential weight of the unborn baby and argued for a renewed sense of "moral gravity,"

> Clinging to a rhetoric about abortion in which there
> is no life and no death, we entangle our beliefs in a
> series of self-delusions, fibs and evasions. . . . We need
> to contextualize the fight to defend abortion rights
> within a moral framework that admits that the death
> of a fetus is a real death.[50]

Wolf's article generated heated anger within the feminist community, and the denial of the humanity of the unborn has, if anything, deepened. Rejected by those Wolf intended to reach, her challenge, therefore, applies all that much more keenly to the church. If we as a community of believers consistently acknowledge that "the death of a fetus is a real death," the role of the church becomes much more clear and unambiguous; it becomes more essential and meaningful.

Grief requires ministry. Questions of recompense, redemption, and reconciliation are not addressed at the ballot box.

If we perceive this issue—because it is contentious—as being merely political and outside the purview of the church, we are leaving a gaping vacuum. The reality of death is revealed through the grief that cannot be denied. And abortion activists continue trying to find ways to categorize and cauterize it. Jennifer Baumgardner, the "I had an abortion" T-shirt activist, also coauthored *Abortion and Life*, a book that, like Naomi Wolf's essay, tries to square the circle of women's pain after abortion. In it they ask, but do not answer, *"What do you do if a patient wants to baptize the remains?"* They later go on to suggest a shift in symbolism, from coat hangers to angels' wings, "to indicate the thousands of women who have abortions and yet believe that a fetus has a soul and is watching over them."[51]

This is a clarion call to the church. The saving power of grace is the only antidote to the corrosive effect of grief and shame. And we have this grace in abundance. So the church must not dismiss the issue as political, masking the light of the gospel. Instead, the church must push back the darkness, unapologetically affirming the destructive realities of abortion and relentlessly proclaiming the better hope found in the grace-filled gospel of Jesus.

Power in Place of Grief

Mary Elizabeth Williams wrote in *Salon* magazine, "I would put the life of the mother over the life of a fetus every single time. Even if I still need to acknowledge my conviction that the fetus is indeed a life. A life worth sacrificing."[52]

Of course not every woman necessarily feels grief after her abortion. Grief's alter ego is defiance. And the protest of the defiant soul is power.

Here is the central premise of today's feminism: that abortion, in its guise as "reproductive freedom" is the irreducible minimum of feminine empowerment. A leader of the "Third Wave" of feminism, Rebecca Walker, the daughter of Alice Walker, the author of *The Color Purple*, wrote an essay in *Harper's*, addressing her comments to younger women, and outlining the feminist conception of reproductive-rights-as-power,

> I hope that the speech I am going to give you will
> encourage you to see that your abortion can be a

rebellious and empowering act. It is an act through which you can assert yourself, one which can enable you to feel more connected to women around the world. It is a surgical operation with a mission.

My hope is that after your abortion, you will commit some part of your life to making sure that others are able to claim their own rights. By doing this, you will use your abortion to connect with women everywhere. You will connect your very special personal with the very important political, and you will begin to know your own power.[53]

The rationale for abortion rights has subtly, but significantly shifted over time. For decades, the post-modern feminist movement has pursued brilliant, disciplined messaging. They clothed their agenda as being about "equal rights" for women, and they've consistently framed the abortion issue using the appealing, unassailable, all-American rhetoric of "choice" and "privacy." However, in the early '90s, subtly and effectively, they began deploying a subtext, carefully marketing a new theme into the American collective subconscious. Unrecognized by most people living normal, everyday lives, the fulcrum for abortion rights has shifted to rest on a question of feminine empowerment.

President Obama's articulation of his support for "choice" during his first presidential campaign—as he was introducing himself to the American voter—provides a quintessentially smooth example of the "power" framework for abortion,

> A woman's ability to decide how many children to have and when, without interference from the government, is one of the most fundamental rights we possess. It is not just an issue of choice, but equality and opportunity for all women.[54]

We need to take careful note, however, that this worldview is deployed on multiple levels; there is far more to it than mere marketing. The messaging on women and power has moved in concert with the underlying legal strategy defending abortion rights. The legal rationale for "reproductive freedom" has evolved significantly over time. In the 1992 decision, *Casey v. Planned Parenthood,* the Court asserted that we must tolerate abortion because of a "reliance interest"—women have come to rely on abortion to maintain their position and advancement in society. Justice Kennedy wrote for the majority in *Casey* that,

> [F]or two decades of economic and social developments, people have organized intimate relationships and made choices that define their views of themselves and their places in society, *in reliance on* the availability of abortion in the event that contraception should fail. The ability of women to participate

equally in the economic and social life of the Nation
has been facilitated by their ability to control their
reproductive lives.[55]

This notion that women must have access to abortion—
for health, for well-being, for power, for self-actualization, for
career advancement—has come to permeate feminist thought.
In fact, the legal arm of the feminist movement, the Center for
Reproductive Rights states this explicitly in their self-definition.
"Reproductive rights, the foundation for women's self-determination over their bodies and sexual lives," the Center's website
explains, "are critical to women's equality and to ensuring global
progress toward just and democratic societies."

In fact, the Center's connection between "reproductive
rights" and democracy illustrates just how foundational abortion has become to the feminist philosophical edifice. This
connective tissue is also now woven into feminist jurisprudence.
For example, Justice Ruth Bader Ginsburg, dissenting from the
Supreme Court's decision to uphold the ban on partial-birth
abortions in *Gonzales v. Carhart* wrote that women cannot "enjoy
equal citizenship stature" without abortion on demand. Abortion
as an essential precursor to citizenship? The entire feminist ideo-
logical edifice now rests on the right to abortion in a way little
recognized by the pro-life movement, despite a consistent public
articulation by the feminist movement.

Engaging Women

Seen in this light—that abortion has produced a corrupted and warped view of women's power in today's culture, and that women are experiencing spiritual destruction through the experience of abortion—the mandate for church engagement is clear. And the church must engage with both women themselves and the culture at large. First, the church can move forward, confident in the necessity of cultural engagement, if it begins with a clear understanding that abortion is—first and foremost—an issue with deep theological significance, which is manifest in the form of women's health and well-being. Second, effective engagement will require further recognition of the evolution of abortion as a theological issue with profound cultural significance. Christians must understand the gravity of framing abortion as an issue of women's "reproductive rights." This label has far-reaching meaning related to a woman's worth as a person and human being, her self-fulfillment, career aspirations, and perception of equality, power, and opportunity. To engage requires us to understand. Our mandate is to speak the truth . . . about abortion, and about the significant and deeply flawed arguments advanced by abortion advocates.

As the old feminist slogan declares: *The personal is political.* The bridge between these two realms is the church. Throughout history, while not perfect, the church has advanced the cause of human rights. When the state has failed the downtrodden, the church has served as the central mediating institution, offering the eternal perspective as a countervailing narrative against the unbridled human quest for temporal power. Paul's admonition to us that "There is no Jew or Greek, slave or free, male or female; for you are all one in Christ Jesus" (Gal. 3:28) is the only foundation for an enduring counterargument to the individualistic isolation that undergirds and sustains abortion.

How then should we engage? A recent survey, conducted by LifeWay Research and sponsored by Care Net, a national consortium of pregnancy care centers, provides insight. Perhaps most importantly, the survey of more than a thousand post-abortive women revealed that church women are a significant proportion of those who choose abortion. *At the time of their first abortion, 37 percent of women were attending a Christian church once a month or more.* Among these women, roughly a third expected their churches to be judgmental or condemning. Another third of the women (28 percent) expected their churches to be helpful. Over half (54 percent) of woman who have had an abortion think that churches oversimplify decisions about pregnancy options.[56]

This underscores a common sense intuition that, regardless of how the church actually responds, women are preemptively on the defensive. A full 65 percent believe the church judges and gossips about single women who are pregnant. More than half would not recommend that a woman in an unplanned pregnancy discuss her options with someone at a local church.

The survey provides much more detail. But the important messages for the church can be summarized this way: Regular churchgoers facing an unplanned pregnancy expect that they would receive good information and help from the church, however they don't talk to anyone at church because they believe it will result in condemnation, judgmental attitudes, and gossip. They don't expect the church to understand the complications and ramifications of an unplanned pregnancy; they think the church will oversimplify the problems they face.

Knowing that these expectations exist as a barrier to ministry, focusing on opening up a line of communication with women is critical. Local churches should be known as centers of grace and refuge. While always affirming a biblical sexual ethic, a local church should be the safest possible place for a woman to disclose an unplanned pregnancy. When women considering abortion won't let the church know about their unplanned pregnancy or their abortion decision, the church cannot engage, and it loses an opportunity to reach a large segment of its members on a critical spiritual issue. This is the responsibility of the whole church. Pastors and church leaders should strive to foster this culture of grace in local churches. And church members are essential in supporting and caring for women or couples challenged by a pregnancy and considering abortion.

One survey finding that should surprise no one is that women facing an unplanned pregnancy are greatly influenced by the father of the baby. More than any other person, the survey participants relied on the reactions of the child's father. However, in the culture as a whole, the father is erased from the abortion picture, pushed out of the frame. Although he's been airbrushed out of the politicized "my body, my choice" discussion, the father is very real to the mother. He's a real person. Publicly, an off-stage actor. Privately, one-half of the baby's DNA.

He may be invisible politically, and legally, but he is more than a ghost to the woman. The famous rap artist Nicki Minaj had an abortion when she was fifteen years old. The pain of that experience permeates her 2008 single "Autobiography," where she asks the baby to forgive her,

> *Please baby forgive me, mommy was young . . .*
> *I adhere to the nonsense*
> *Listened to people who told me I wasn't ready for you*
> *But how [. . .] would they know what I was ready to do*
> *And of course it wasn't your fault*
> *It's like I feel it in the air,*
> *I hear you saying "mommy don't cry,*
> *Can't you see I'm right here?"*
> *I gotta let you know what you mean to me*
> *When I'm sleeping I see you in my dreams with me*

Wish I could touch your little face
Or just hold your little hand
If it's part of God's plan,
Maybe we can meet again

In a 2015 *Rolling Stone* profile, Minaj told the reporter, "It was the hardest thing I have ever gone through. It has haunted me all my life."[57] And the father, her "first love," is very real to her. In a single called "All Things Go" on her *The Pinkprint* album, she returns again to the abortion, and she names the father: "My child with Aaron, would've been sixteen any minute."[58] Almost two decades later, the grief is still there.

The way that Minaj presents herself, and how she talks about her abortion, is a microcosm of the issues and challenges involved with engaging the issue. We see both the grief and the focus on female empowerment. "I stand for girls wanting to be sexy and dance," Minaj told *Rolling Stone*, "but also having a strong sense of themselves."[59] This raw desire for female empowerment is bracketed by an enduring grief over abortion and the loss of the "first love." This begs the question: where does the strong sense of self come from? In the culture today, whether it's Nicki Minaj or Rebecca Walker, or Lena Dunham or Hillary Clinton, the message is a rootless, ephemeral "Love Yourself" mantra that devolves into a hyper-sexualization of all things feminine. The end result is a commodification of female sexuality that necessitates abortion as an integral feature of a worldview based on the lone, and lonely, self.

The church must respond. Abortion is the lynchpin of the alternate narrative of Life and Truth. It usually exists unacknowledged for this central philosophical-religious role, masquerading as merely another "political issue." Without the knowledge and reality of God's enduring love for each person—whether Jew or Gentile, slave or free, male or female—the world is an alien and hostile place where each individual struggles for validation and power with weak, ineffective tools. So the church must stand ready to respond to both the grieving and the embattled. We must point toward the incredible grace and forgiveness available through the gospel. We must point toward the finished work of Christ that allows the grieving and lost to experience His love.

A Better Hope

In her passionate and heart-breaking poem, "I Think She Was a She,"[60] Scottish performance artist Leyla Josephine declares, "I am not ashamed" as she describes why she had an abortion.

She could have been born.
I would have made sure that we had a space on
the wall to measure her height as she grew.
I would have made sure I was a good mother to look up to.

> *But I would have supported her right to choose.*
> *To choose a life for herself, a path for herself.*
> *I would have died for that right, just like she died for mine.*
> **I'm sorry but you came at the wrong time.**
> *I am not ashamed. I am not ashamed. I am not ashamed.*

Acknowledging the humanity of her baby. She's a she. And she could have been born. But "you came at the wrong time." Even with the defiant refrain, *I am not ashamed, not ashamed, not ashamed*, the sorrow screams through every line. Even while masquerading as an abortion rights manifesto, it's a chronicling of how the baby haunts her. She concludes the poem with bravado, "This is my story and it will not be written in pencil and erased with guilt. It will be written in pain and spoken in courage."

A poem is an attempt to process pain and regret. But it does not have the hope of faith, the power of repentance, and the forgiveness that makes everything new and brings meaning to all of life.

> *I had to carve down that little cherry tree*
> *that had rooted itself in my blood and blossomed in my brain.*
> *A responsibility I didn't have the energy or age to maintain.*
> *The branches casting shadows over the rest of the garden.*
> *The bark causing my thoughts, my heart to harden.*
> *I am not ashamed. I am not ashamed. I am not ashamed.*
> *It's a hollowness, that feels full, a numbness that feels heavy.*

Today's young people live in a complex world. They are growing up in a culture awash in everyday pornography that has become so commonplace and ubiquitous that even *Playboy* magazine has backed away from nudity in a quest for originality. But some things remain resolutely unchanging: a young woman who is pregnant and alone is vulnerable, exposed, and faces cultural approbation. While the strictures against premarital sex have loosened, those against pregnancy have not. The pressures toward abortion remain intense. The church needs to persevere with a biblically-grounded, pro-life message that addresses the needs of a generation used to relying on Planned Parenthood, rather than the church—a generation that shapes its morals via culture rather than conviction, by physical impulses rather than biblical principles. And this is done by taking a holistic approach to the issue. From sermons to Sunday school, from hosting baby showers to supporting pregnancy care centers, to offering counseling, housing, and financial support, local churches are best situated to engage authentically, comprehensively, and urgently.

The LifeWay survey showed that women who regularly attend church understand that the church offers compassionate help and information. Regular attendees were approximately four times more likely to view the church favorably and to expect caring, practical, and loving help from its members. That affirmation of the ministry of the church is needed when the church is regularly portrayed as irrelevant and no longer essential in the public square. The women of the survey affirmed the important role of church ministry in meeting people where they are and helping them move to where God wants them to be—where He formed them, for true self-realization: to thrive, be fulfilled and empowered for a life of meaning and significance.

Women who are contemplating an abortion, and those who have been harmed by abortion, need hope, support, and clear direction. They need to sense that the hopelessness and lack of choice they feel that drives them to abortion is recognized. They need to feel and experience the love and acceptance of the people of God in tangible ways. They need to know that the church understands that "choosing life" in real life is not a Hallmark card or a bumper sticker. And they need the church to come alongside them as they face the difficulties of pregnancy and the challenges of motherhood.

The most pernicious lie that the abortion industry tells is the fiction that they are on the side of women and that they stand for feminine power. Because in truth, their actual message is one of weakness. They tell young women, "You aren't ready." When a woman is at her lowest point of desperation, they say, "You can't do it." Nicki Minaj called their refrain for what it is, nonsense.

I adhere to the nonsense
Listened to people who told me I wasn't ready for you
But how [. . .] would they know what I was ready to do

This is the mission for the church, to hold out the alternate story. To encourage and support a vision of hope. To tell women they can face the future.

Because Leyla Josephine is right.

She could have been born.

Discussion Questions

1. Given that women who have had abortions think that the church community would react negatively if they asked about pregnancy options, how can we make women feel more comfortable opening up to seek help during an unplanned pregnancy?

2. What messages is Leyla Josephine trying to communicate in her poem when she claims that she is "not ashamed" of her abortion, given the juxtaposition between the pain she describes and her defense of abortion? How does her posture compare with what Nicki Minaj says about her abortion? With Rebecca Walker?

3. How can we reach men who have been affected by abortion? How can we better connect them to the conversation prior to the abortion?

4. Where should the church draw the line between upholding a biblical worldview valuing life and still communicate grace and forgiveness to both women and men who have chosen abortion in their past?

5. How can the church engage the cultural conversation
    about women, power, and their place in society? Do you
    think women "rely on" abortion as Justice Kennedy said
    in *Casey v. Planned Parenthood*?

CHAPTER

5

What Does the Culture Say?

C. Ben Mitchell

"IN THOSE DAYS THERE WAS NO KING IN ISRAEL; EVERYONE did whatever he wanted" (Judg. 21:25).

No one can adequately comprehend the current state of the abortion debate in America without understanding the trajectory that has led to it. Without question, American culture has been shaped—as Western civilization has been shaped—by the Judeo-Christian belief in the sanctity of human life. Both Jews and Christians have affirmed historically that human beings are made in the image of God *(imago Dei)* and, therefore, possess lives worthy of respect and protection. The *imago Dei* is the foundation for the West's understanding of human dignity, human rights, and what some have called human exceptionalism. This view of the nature of human beings led early Christians to reject infanticide, the brutality of the gladiatorial games, and the subjugation of women. Respect for human life also motivated these early Christians to establish orphanages, hospitals, and other forms of humanitarian aid.

Later in our history, the sacred nature of human life was enshrined in the documents of the American founding. The signers of the United States Declaration of Independence confessed: "We hold these truths to be self-evident, that all men are created equal, that they are endowed by their Creator with certain unalienable Rights, that among these are Life, Liberty and the pursuit of Happiness." The recognition that human beings are made in the image of God has a direct bearing on the history of abortion and other assaults on human life.

During the eighteenth and nineteenth centuries, for instance, abortions were illegal after the period of fetal development then called "quickening," the point at which a woman could feel the baby's movements inside her body. The law protected the unborn once there was clear evidence that he or she was alive. Living members of the human species, even those in the womb, were thus protected in law and respected by culture. Even many feminists of the day were outspoken opponents of abortion.

Suffragists such as Susan B. Anthony, Jane Addams, and Louisa May Alcott joined their voices with others who decried abortion in the late nineteenth century.

Despite these notable examples of the pro-life culture in the West, American chattel of slavery and the Holocaust represented horrific deviations in human history. These atrocities were the result of one group of humans reducing another group of humans to sub-human status. However, the fact that these practices were eventually repudiated on the grounds that they violated human dignity, underscores the point that Western civilization was built on the understanding that human life is sacred. That is, the cultural reformation in both America and Germany were made possible because of this enduring affirmation that every human being, regardless of ethnicity, ability, or culture, should be free from the threat of unjustifiable harm. The American quest for economic advantage through the use of human slaves, and the Nazi quest for national superiority through the extermination of so-called human "defectives," could not ultimately trump the sanctity of every human life. Post-Civil War Reconstruction in America and the Nuremberg Trials in Germany were correctives to cultures gone mad. Inhabiting a Christian worldview makes self-correction both possible and necessary at times.

From Culture of Life to Culture of Self

Another seismic shift in the culture began to rock American society by the late 1950s and early 1960s. In this case, the quest for personal satisfaction based on one's individual desires became the trump card for making life's decisions. Personal autonomy—individual choice—became the end-all for decision making. As the emphasis on individualism was growing, the sexual revolution was toppling the social mores of the culture with respect to sex, marriage, and the family.

Consider for a moment the prevailing perspective on traditional marriage in 1950:

- One should refrain from sexual activity until marriage (i.e., the wedding night).
- An essential and normal purpose of marriage is to produce children.
- One should refrain from sexual activity with anyone but one's spouse.
- One should choose a spouse from the opposite sex.
- The marital estate is intended to be a permanent love relationship.

Today, every plank of this tradition has undergone radical revision.

- Courtship is dying; the "hook-up culture" is in.

- Cohabitation is a growing problem.
- Marriage between a man and woman is disintegrating.
- Pornography is pandemic.
- Sexual abuse is daily news, including among the clergy.
- The "adult toys" industry is mainstream.
- The best-seller *Fifty Shades of Grey* popularizes "mommy porn."
- No-fault divorce is rampant.
- Children are suffering from the disintegration of the family at a higher rate than ever before.
- Polyamory is becoming increasingly acceptable.
- Same-sex marriage is currently legal.

By any definition of social change, what has been happening in American culture since the 1960s is not an evolution, but a revolution. How did such radical change happen in such a short period of time?

The Long March to Nowhere

In his splendid volume *The Long March: How the Cultural Revolution of the 1960s Changed America*, cultural analyst and art critic Roger Kimball observed: "The movement for sexual 'liberation' (not to say outright debauchery) occupies a prominent place in the etiology of this revolution, as does the mainstreaming of the drug culture and its attendant pathologies. Indeed, the two are related. Both are expressions of the narcissistic hedonism that was an important ingredient of the counterculture from its development in the 1950s."[61]

Narcissistic hedonism—the pursuit of personal, self-gratification as the aim of life—is now the predominant worldview shaping our culture. As Kimball said, "The Age of Aquarius did not end when the last electric guitar was unplugged at Woodstock. It lives on in our values and habits, in our tastes, pleasures, and aspirations. It lives on especially in our educational and cultural institutions, and in the degraded pop culture that permeates our lives like a corrosive fog."[62]

He went on to observe,

> That ideology has insinuated itself, disastrously, into the curricula of our schools and colleges; it has significantly altered the texture of sexual relations and family life; it has played havoc with the authority of the churches and other repositories of moral wisdom; it has undermined the claims of civic virtue and our national self-understanding; it has degraded the media, the entertainment industry, and popular culture; it has helped to subvert museums and other institutions entrusted with preserving and transmitting high culture. It has even, most poignantly, addled our hearts and innermost assumptions about

what counts as the good life: it has perverted our
dreams as much as it has prevented us from attaining
them.[63]

With this new worldview coming into vogue, attitudes about
abortion also mutated. Narcissistic hedonism fanned the flames
of sexual promiscuity and the so-called free-love movement,
which was neither free nor loving in reality. Sexual liberation
meant not only that individuals could choose for themselves if
and when they had sex, but they could also determine for themselves whether and how they should deal with the consequences
of sex. If they chose to experience sex without benefit of marriage, that was their own business. If they chose to marry either
before or after having sex, that was their own business. If they
chose not to marry at all, that was their own business. Sex was
between consenting adults. It was their own business. If the individuals involved are self-fulfilled, indulging their own desires,
and not harming others, the behavior was viewed as permissible,
the rest of the culture be damned. But as we have just seen there
were harms to others.

Normal human biology posed one problem. The union of
a man and woman in an act of sexual intimacy often results in
pregnancy. The potential of unwanted offspring posed a serious
threat to the gratification of personal desire without consequences. After all, children were a real and distinct consequence
of sexual intimacy. What does one do about those consequences?

The Abortion Culture

Abortion offered one answer. According to the Guttmacher Institute, the polling arm of Planned Parenthood, a pro-abortion organization, "the number of illegal abortions in the 1950s and 1960s ranged from 200,000 to 1.2 million per year." By the 1970s the acids of the sexual revolution had eaten away at the sanctity of human life doctrine to the degree that the United States Supreme Court ruled in *Roe v. Wade* (1973) and *Doe v. Bolton* (1973) that abortion would be legal in nearly any situation. From 1973 to 2015, there have been a staggering 57.7 million abortions. More people have died from abortion than the entire US population of 1880.

As horrible as the abortion crisis is, it would be wrong to think that this is what most women desire deep down. Frederica Mathews-Green was a radical feminist who later came to faith in Christ. When she reflected on her own thoughts about abortion, she said,

> For years we've had the circular idea that, sure, abortion kills babies, but it's what women want. But we know that it's not what women want, not in any reasonable sense of the word. It's what women choose when they run out of choices. They want it like a cancer patient wants to lose a breast. But this is even worse, because what you lose is your own child. Time doesn't make this dandy. Abortion hurts women and

breaks their hearts. We've seen our friend's face, so we know.[64]

Ironically, in the name of choice and self-fulfillment, women's choices are restricted and they are left far less than fulfilled. Although sexual intimacy has definite consequences, it does not have to mean a death sentence for an unborn child and a lifetime of guilt and regret for a woman.

The Contraceptive Culture

The contraceptive pill offered another answer to the problem of unwanted pregnancy. Birth control has been available since ancient times. Most methods are relatively unreliable. According to the US Centers for Disease Control and Prevention, even if used correctly, condoms fail to prevent pregnancy about 18 percent of the time, and the diaphragm 12 percent of the time.

In the early twentieth century, feminists like Margaret Sanger, the founder of Planned Parenthood, agitated for more acceptable and reliable birth control to support what she called "voluntary motherhood." Despite the fact that she was both a eugenicist and racist, Sanger is hailed by many today as a champion of a woman's right to choose if, when, and with whom to have children. Again, self-determination has trumped all other concerns.

More than fifty years ago, in an effort to treat infertility, a physician named John Rock inadvertently invented the contraceptive pill. The pill "rearranged the furniture of human relations in ways that we have argued about ever since," said executive editor of *TIME* magazine, Nancy Gibbs, in her contraception advocacy book, *Love, Sex, Freedom and the Paradox of the Pill: A Brief History of Birth Control.* The pill both aided and abetted the revolution of the 1960s by contributing to the myth that there could be such a thing as "free sex"—sexual intercourse free of consequences. Men and women came to believe that the pill was a liberator. And, unfortunately, even many evangelical Christians embraced the pill as yet another technological advance.

Albert Mohler, president of The Southern Baptist Theological Seminary, has lamented,

> Evangelicals were not on the front lines of the abortion revolution. I think the contraceptive revolution caught Evangelicals by surprise. We bought into a mentality of control. We welcomed the polio vaccine and penicillin and just received the Pill as one more medical advance.[65]

Truth and Consequences

In reality, of course, ideas—and choices rooted in those ideas—do have consequences. The cultural revolution gave birth to the sexual revolution, and the culture of life has given way to a culture of death. Abortion and contraception are largely being used for damage control and the result is that the unborn die. Furthermore, at the other end of life, the cultural revolution is reverberating through the medical culture through the legalization of physician-assisted suicide in several US states. Abortion and assisted suicide are not unrelated. What a person believes about the value of human beings at the beginning of life has profound implications for what one believes about the value of human beings at the end of life. And the consequences are equally dire, men and women made in God's image and likeness die at their own hands with the complicity of other men and women, doctors and nurses, who are meant to save life. Doctors and nurses have an ethical duty to do what they can to alleviate suffering, but they should not knowingly involve themselves in the active death of a patient, even if the patient requests it. Caregivers must not be complicit in killing their patients. Yet the assisted suicide juggernaut continues to turn medicine upside down.

Creating a Counterrevolution of Christian Hospitality

Against this bleak backdrop, some encouraging things are happening, especially among Christians. Just as early Christians responded to their own cultural crisis by creating orphanages, hospitals, and repudiating a cultural of barbarism, Christians today are responding to this current cultural crisis. The Christian faith welcomes "the other," whether he is a homeless man in Seattle, a parentless child in Dallas, or an unborn baby in the womb in Pensacola. Hospitality has always been a hallmark of biblical faith.

Many Christians are recommitting themselves to the importance of traditional marriage. When a man and woman cleave to one another in the one-flesh relationship of covenant marriage, this is hospitality. Sex within the sphere of the marital union of a man and woman is a blessing from God and a clearly human good. We know this not only from Scripture, but numerous studies show by nearly any metric one chooses that marriage is good for men, women, and children. What is good for men, women, and children is good for our culture and contributes to human flourishing.

Christians are also active in the creation and growth of pregnancy care centers that provide women with truthful information about pregnancy and offer other options than abortion. Founded in 1975, Care Net supports one of the largest networks of pregnancy centers in North America and runs the nation's only real-time call center providing pregnancy decision coaching. According to their "Impact Report," over a six-year period Care Net pregnancy centers provided 579,322 free ultrasound scans, 1.8 million free pregnancy tests, and 723,597 individuals received parenting support and education. Moreover, more than one million people heard the gospel of Jesus through the work of the centers. On a local level, the Pregnancy Care Center in Plant City, Florida, sees six hundred clients visit per month. In addition to pregnancy testing and child care information, thirty to thirty-five women participate in Bible study classes that are offered three times per week. This is Christian hospitality at work.

The apostle James wrote that "pure and undefiled religion before our God and Father is this: to look after orphans and widows in their distress and to keep oneself unstained by the world" (James 1:27). So, growing numbers of Catholic and evangelical Christians are adopting children as an expression of Christian hospitality. According to one Barna study, Christians are more than twice as likely to adopt a child as non-Christians. Five percent of practicing Christians have adopted children and 3 percent are foster parents. Agencies like Bethany Christian Services specialize in helping Christians adopt. Located in thirty-six states and numerous countries in the world, their services include adoption, foster care, and pregnancy counseling.

Christian hospitality is leading increasing numbers of Christians to rethink contraception. Historically, Roman Catholic doctrine has taught that it is wrong to use contraception to prevent new human beings from coming into existence. Of course, this does not mean that every couple must have as many children as possible. In his encyclical letter *Humanae Vitae*, Pope Paul VI said,

> If therefore there are well-grounded reasons for spacing births, arising from the physical or psychological condition of husband or wife, or from external circumstances, the Church teaches that married people may then take advantage of the natural cycles immanent in the reproductive system and engage in marital intercourse only during those times that are infertile, thus controlling birth in a way which does not in the least offend the moral principles which we have just explained. (HV 16)

So *Humanae Vitae*, we might say, calls for procreative hospitality. New human lives are a gift from God and should be received with thanksgiving.

The rejection of the contraceptive culture is not limited to Catholics. Evangelicals and other Protestants are also reconsidering the use of contraceptives, especially those that may have abortion-causing effects. In their book *Open Embrace: A Protestant Couple Rethinks Contraception*, Sam and Bethany Torode describe the theological and practical reasons many couples are choosing not to use the pill and other contraceptives. The sanctity of human life, the one-flesh relationship between a husband and wife, the nature of sexual intimacy, and the reality of our embodiment show, the authors argue, that Christians should break from their cultural captivity to create hospitable communities where children are welcomed on their own terms.

Three Pillars of a Decent Society

Despite these very encouraging countercultural moves, it is important to remember what is at stake. Robert P. George is McCormick Professor of Jurisprudence at Princeton University. He has argued that any healthy society will rest upon three pillars. *The first is respect for the human person.* "A society that does not nurture respect for the human person—beginning with the child in the womb and including the mentally and physically impaired and the frail elderly—will sooner or later (probably sooner) come to regard human beings as mere cogs in the larger social wheel whose dignity and well-being may legitimately be sacrificed for the sake of collectivity."[66]

The second pillar of a decent society is the institution of the family, based on the marital commitment of husband and wife. "Where families fail to form, or many break down," says George, "the effective transmission of the virtues of honesty, civility, self-restraint, concern for the welfare of others, justice, compassion, and personal responsibility will be imperiled."[67]

A fair and effective system of law and government is the third pillar of a decent society. Law serves both an ordering and corrective function. We are not virtuous all of the time, so the law is a corrective force in a just society. Not only so, but in order to sustain business, commerce, and enforce contracts, we need law to provide structure and order to our common life. Assaults on the rule of law in American culture are daily in the news. Each of these pillars have provided powerful resistance to the culture of death, but, today, each of them have serious fractures and may be in danger of collapse.

Conclusion

The revolution is, most likely, not over yet. Abortion on demand and voluntary childlessness through contraception are signs of a culture in the throes of death. It cannot long survive. The question to which only God knows the answer is how much more decadent, debauched, and degenerate will the culture become before the collapse. But because faithful Christians live in hope that is not tethered to a particular time and particular place, we can be agents of the gospel of Jesus Christ who serve the weak, vulnerable, homeless, penniless, born, and unborn, for the glory of God.

The fortunes of the Christian church are not dependent on the moral health of the United States, but the moral health of the United States is dependent on the fidelity of God's people, living, worshipping, and serving as God's people. This is nothing new. This is how it was in those earlier days when the church was young. Like those New Testament believers, we are exiles and sojourners. We should continue to work toward the rehabilitation of a decent and dynamic culture, but we realize it may be too late to turn it around apart from another Great Awakening, or the return of the King of kings and Lord of lords, Jesus the risen Messiah.

Should Christians remain active in the political sphere as long as they can? Of course we should. We are to be good citizens. But our trust must not be placed in political maneuvering or power politics. As the psalmist reminds us, "Some trust in chariots and some in horses, but we trust in the name of the LORD our God" (Ps. 20:7 ESV).

Discussion Questions

1. In addition to abortion and contraception, what are other signs of a culture of death?
2. What are other ways of cultivating a culture of respect for human life? How does being created in the image of God inform our understanding of human dignity?
3. What new ministry should you and your church develop for the weak and vulnerable of your neighborhood?
4. In the midst of a culture of death, what are some practical ways Christians can engage in the "counterrevolution" of

Christian hospitality? What kind of effect could this have on the broader culture?

5. What are the three pillars of a decent society? What condition are these pillars in today, and how can a Christian worldview provide correctives?

Have You Chosen Abortion?

Dear Friend,

You are not alone. As I shared in my opening letter, I have been where you are. I have felt the intense grief, anguish, and shame that you feel. I aborted my first baby thirty-three years ago when I was just eighteen years old. I have felt the deep sorrow in knowing I will never hold and love my baby on this earth. I have struggled with the "if only" complex: *if only I would have known how much I already loved you, if only I fought for your life, if only I could go back and choose to save you!* But, I have found forgiveness and hope in Jesus Christ alone! I must start with that fact so that you will know that you, too, can experience the same freedom and joy that I now have in Jesus Christ.

The circumstances surrounding our abortion experiences may be different, but I believe the pain of choosing to end our child's lives through abortion is the same. It is extremely difficult for a woman to process the fear, anger, sadness, and guilt surrounding her abortion experience. Women often feel isolated because they fear sharing their pain with others. However, I would greatly encourage you to contact your local church or crisis pregnancy center for help. Most of these centers offer a Bible study for women who regret their abortion to help them find freedom from their guilt and shame.

I went through one of these Bible studies called "Forgiven and Set Free" by Linda Cochrane with a group of women many years ago and have been leading other women through them for twenty-five years. I have seen God miraculously heal women, as only He can. There is nothing that any human can do or say to heal us from this pain, but God, in His unfathomable mercy, chooses to heal us and set us free from our grief, guilt, and shame, as we trust Him. God doesn't stop there! He not only sets us free but He replaces the grief with pure joy! We find hope that we will be reunited with our children one day in heaven at our Savior's feet!

I want you to know and believe that you, too, can experience healing and forgiveness in Jesus Christ. Abortion is a sin that cuts to the very core of who God created you to be as a woman. Therefore, it is only God who can restore you to complete wholeness in Him! And, He delights in showing mercy to His children. You only need to be willing and ready to accept it and turn to Jesus Christ in repentance. He is waiting patiently for you. He loves you and desires to set you free! John 8:36 states: "Therefore, if the Son sets you free, you really will be free."

A Fellow Mother

ADDITIONAL READING

Abortion: A Rational Look at an Emotional Issue by R. C. Sproul

Pro-Life Answers to Pro-Choice Arguments (Expanded & Updated) by Randy Alcorn

Why Pro-Life? Caring for the Unborn and Their Mothers by Randy Alcorn

Healing after Abortion: God's Mercy Is for You by David Powlison

A Compassionate Call to Counter Culture in a World of Abortion by David Platt

Abortion Rites: A Social History of Abortion in America by Marvin Olasky

ACKNOWLEDGMENTS

TO THE MANY HANDS INSIDE AND OUTSIDE THE ERLC, WE thank you for your help and assistance on this book. The ERLC team provided joyful encouragement in the planning and execution of this series, and without them, it would never have gotten off the ground. We want to also personally thank Phillip Bethancourt who was a major visionary behind this project. We'd also like to thank Jennifer Lyell and Devin Maddox at B&H, our publisher, for their work in guiding us through this process.

ABOUT THE ERLC

THE ERLC IS DEDICATED TO ENGAGING THE CULTURE WITH the gospel of Jesus Christ and speaking to issues in the public square for the protection of religious liberty and human flourishing. Our vision can be summed up in three words: kingdom, culture, and mission.

Since its inception, the ERLC has been defined around a holistic vision of the kingdom of God, leading the culture to change within the church itself and then as the church addresses the world. The ERLC has offices in Washington, DC, and Nashville, Tennessee.

ABOUT THE CONTRIBUTORS

James M. Hamilton Jr. is professor of biblical Theology at The Southern Baptist Theological Seminary and pastor of Kenwood Baptist Church in Louisville, Kentucky.

Matt Chandler is the lead pastor of Teaching at The Village Church in Flower Mound, Texas, and president of the Acts 29 Network. He speaks at conferences throughout the world and is the author of multiple books including *The Explicit Gospel*.

Karen Swallow Prior is professor of English at Liberty University, a research fellow with the Ethics and Religious Liberty Commission, and author of *Fierce Convictions: The Extraordinary Life of Hannah More—Poet, Reformer, Abolitionist*.

Charmaine Crouse Yoest is an author and commentator who lives in the Washington, DC, area. She began her career in the Reagan White House, has a Ph.D. from the University of Virginia, and has been involved in the pro-life movement for over three decades.

C. Ben Mitchell, PhD, is provost and vice president of academic affairs at Union University with campuses in Jackson, Germantown, and Hendersonville, Tennessee. He also serves as Graves Professor of Moral Philosophy.

NOTES

1. For a full study, see Richard Lints, *Identity and Idolatry: The Image of God and Its Inversion*, NSBT (Downers Grove, IL: InterVarsity, 2015).

2. See further James M. Hamilton, *God's Glory in Salvation through Judgment: A Biblical Theology* (Wheaton, IL: Crossway, 2010).

3. 3D ultrasound was copyrighted in 1987 by Olaf T. Von Ramm and Stephen W. Smith, http://worldwide.espacenet.com/publication Details/biblio?CC=US&NR=4694434&KC=&FT=E&locale=en_EP.

4. See https://www.ehd.org/movies.php?mov_id=21.

5. See https://www.ehd.org/movies.php?mov_id=248.

6. See https://www.ehd.org/movies.php?mov_id=41; https://www.ehd.org/movies.php?mov_id=42.

7. See https://www.ehd.org/movies.php?mov_id=41.

8. See http://ethicscenter.nd.edu/news/57872-public-policy-fellow-maureen-condic-testifies-before-congress; full testimony: http://judiciary.house.gov/_files/hearings/113th/05232013/Condic%2005232013.pdf.

9. See http://www.babycenter.com/0_fetal-development-timeline_10357636.bc.

10. Ibid.

11. See http://www.newsweek.com/babies-born-22-weeks-can-survive-medical-care-new-study-finds-329518.

12. See http://www.guttmacher.org/pubs/fb_induced_abortion.html.

13. See http://www.salon.com/2013/01/23 so_what_if_abortion_ends_life.

14. See http://genetics.thetech.org/ask/ask420.

15. Nicholas Wolterstorff, *Justice Rights and Wrongs* (Princeton: Princeton University Press, 2008), 292.

16. See http://aldf.org/blog/50-states-now-have-felony-animal-cruelty-provisions.

17. See http://www.ncsl.org/research/health/fetal-homicide-state-laws.aspx.

18. See http://www.tertullian.org/articles/reeve_apology.htm.

19. See http://www.ancient-origins.net/history/discovery-mass-baby-grave-under-roman-bathhouse-ashkelon-israel-002399.

20. See http://jewishchristianlit.com/Texts/ANElaws/midAssyrLaws.html.

21. See http://news.bbc.co.uk/2/hi/7654432.stm.

22. Quoted in George Grant, *Third Time Around: A History of the Pro-Life Movement from the First Century to the Present* (Aurora, CO: Wolgelmuth & Hyatt, 1991), 24.

23. See http://www.ccel.org/ccel/schaff/npnf205.x.ii.ii.xxx.html.

24. See http://www.tertullian.org/articles/reeve_apology.htm.

25. See http://caselaw.findlaw.com/us-supreme-court/410/113.html.

26. See https://www.law.cornell.edu/supremecourt/text/410/179.

27. See http://www.lifenews.com/2012/12/20/even-abortion-backers-admit-roe-vs-wade-was-a-terrible-decision.

28. See http://www.deveber.org/text/chapters/Chap16.pdf.

29. See http://choicesaz.com/for-men-only/abortion-recovery-for-men.

30. See http://www.gallup.com/poll/1576/abortion.aspx.

31. See http://www.guttmacher.org/media/nr/2014/02/03.

32. See http://dttefinitions.uslegal.com/f/fetal-homicide%20.

33. http://www.ncsl.org/research/health/fetal-homicide-state-laws.aspx

34. See http://www.guttmacher.org/statecenter/spibs/spib_OAL.pdf.

35. See http://www.worldtribune.com/2014/01/25/how-the-pro-life-movement-is-winning-american-hearts-and-minds.

36. *Christianity Today,* September 2015, 16.

37. See http://www.priestsforlife.org/legislation.

38. See https://books.google.com/books?id=s3FkRrD2KaoC&pg=PA118&lpg=PA118&dq=carl+henry+work+through+civil+authority&source=bl&ots=kBfINTSiYd&sig=P3NTygy0S6_1_UrvcsIvA8pIv0s&hl=en&sa=X&ved=0CCkQ6AEwAmoVChMI_K7TjJvUxwIVgXo-Ch2ITw2w#v=onepage&q=carl%20henry%20work%20through%20civil%20authority&f=false.

39. *Christianity Today,* September 2015, 16.

40. See http://www.nytimes.com/2013/01/05/health/pregnancy-centers-gain-influence-in-anti-abortion-fight.html?_r=0

41. See http://www.nytimes.com/2013/01/05/health/pregnancy-centers-gain-influence-in-anti-abortion-fight.html?_r=0

42. "Artist hanged herself after aborting her twins," *The Telegraph*, February 2, 2008, http://www.telegraph.co.uk/news/uknews/1579455/Artist-hanged-herself-after-aborting-her-twins.html.

43. Dan Gilgoff, "Abortion Foes Circulate Abortion-as-Tonsillectomy Video," *U.S. News and World Report,* July 24, 2009, http://www.usnews.com/news/blogs/god-and-country/2009/07/24/abortion-foes-circulate-abortion-as-tonsillectomy-video https://www.youtube.com/watch?v=v-iQtsuHXjQ.

44. Gilliam Aldrich and Jennifer Baumgardner, "The Shirt," *Speak Out: I Had an Abortion* (documentary film), Screening, February 24, 2009, http://abortionandlife.com/p/the-shirt.

45. Cecile Richards, "Ending the Silence that Fuels Abortion Stigma," *The Abortions Issue,* October 16, 2014, http://www.elle.com/culture/career-politics/a15060/cecile-richards-abortion-stigma.

46. "Summary of Known Health Risks of Abortion," Americans United for Life, No date, http://www.aul.org/wp-content/uploads/2013/08/Summary-of-Known-Health-Risks-of-Abortion.pdf.

47. Meaghan Winter, "My Abortion," *New York Magazine*, November 10, 2013, http://nymag.com/news/features/abortion-stories-2013-11.

48. "Abortion Story: Orlando, FL," *Abortion73.com*, October 9, 2015, http://www.abort73.com/testimony/2083.

49. "Abortion Story: Lakeland, FL," *Abortion73.com*, October 9, 2015, http://www.abort73.com/testimony/2082.

50. Naomi Wolf, "Re-Thinking Pro-Choice Rhetoric," *The New Republic* (Re-Printed by Priests for Life), October 16, 1995, http://www.priestsforlife.org/prochoice/ourbodiesoursouls.htm.

51. Jennifer Baumgardner, *Abortion and Life*, New York: Akashic Books, 2008, 10, http://www.jenniferbaumgardner.net/books-all#/abortion-life.

52. Mary Elizabeth Williams, "So What If Abortion Ends Life?" *Salon Magazine*, January 23, 2013, http://www.salon.com/2013/01/23/so_what_if_abortion_ends_life.

53. Rebecca Walker, untitled article, *Harper's Magazine*, November, 1992, 51, (available only by subscription) http://harpers.org/archive/1992/11.

54. President Barack Obama, "Coveting the Evangelical Vote," *Orange County Register,* August 10, 2008, http://www.ocregister.com/articles/evangelicals-29987-faith-mccain.html.

55. *Planned Parenthood of Southeastern Pa. v. Casey* 505 U.S. 833 (1992), https://supreme.justia.com/cases/federal/us/505/833.

56. "Study of Women who have had an Abortion and Their Views on Church," LifeWay Research: Biblical Solutions for Life, Sponsored by Care Net, November, 2015, www.lifewayresearch.com/files/2015/11/care-net-final-presentation-report-revised.pdf.

57. "Nicki Minaj Is Hip-Hop's Killer Diva: Inside Rolling Stone's New Issue," *Rolling Stone Magazine*, December 30, 2014, http://

www.rollingstone.com/music/news/nicki-minaj-is-hip-hops-killer-diva-inside-rolling-stones-new-issue-20141230.

58. Nicki Minaj, *All Things Go*, Genius.com, http://genius.com/Nicki-minaj-all-things-go-lyrics.

59. "Nicki Minaj Is Hip-Hop's Killer Diva," *Rolling Stone.*

60. Leyla Josephine, "I Think She Was a She," *The Feminist Fatale* Blog, September 21, 2014, https://feministfindings.wordpress.com/tag/leylajosephine.

61. Roger Kimball, *The Long March: How the Cultural Revolution of the 1960s Changed America* (New York City, NY: Encounter Books, 2001), xvi.

62. Ibid., iv.

63. Ibid., xvi.

64. Frederica Mathewes-Green, "Moment of Silence," *Frederica.com*, March 10, 2001, http://frederica.com/writings/moment-of-silence.html.

65. See http://content.time.com/time/magazine/article/0,9171,1983884-5,00.html.

66. Robert P. George, "No Mere Marriage of Convenience: The Unity of Economic and Social Conservatism," *First Things,* November 16, 2012, http://www.firstthings.com/web-exclusives/2012/11/no-mere-marriage-of-convenience-the-unity-of-economic-and-social-conservatism.

67. Ibid.

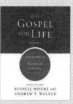
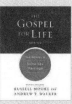
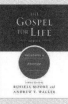
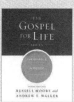